*Oxford in the Twenties*

A selection of books by
CHRISTOPHER HOLLIS

Thomas More
Foreigners Aren't Fools
Death of a Gentleman
Fossett's Memory
Can Parliament Survive?
A Study of George Orwell
Along the Road to Frome
Eton
The Papacy
The Oxford Union
Newman and the Modern World
A History of the Jesuits
The Mind of Chesterton
Parliament and its Sovereignty
The Seven Ages

# OXFORD IN THE TWENTIES

*Recollections of Five Friends*

Christopher Hollis

HEINEMANN : LONDON

William Heinemann Ltd
15 Queen Street, Mayfair, London W1X8BE

LONDON   MELBOURNE   TORONTO
JOHANNESBURG   AUCKLAND


First published in Great Britain 1976
Copyright © by Christopher Hollis 1976


434 34531 8

Printed in Great Britain by
WESTERN PRINTING SERVICES LTD
Bristol

# Contents

# Oxford before the Twenties

O born in days when wits were fresh and clear,
And life ran gaily as the sparkling Thames;
Before this strange disease of modern life,
With its sick hurry, its divided aims.
*The Scholar Gipsy*—Matthew Arnold

The Oxford of the Middle Ages, like all other European Universities, was a religious body. In the mediaeval society it was only the clergy who needed education. The clergyman was not, it is true, necessarily a priest, but all those who performed a task that required reading and writing were in some sort of Orders. Cleric and clerk were interchangeable terms, as were person and parson. With the Renaissance came the notion that it might be desirable for some lay people, and even some women, also to receive education. The sixteenth century in England gave us Thomas More and his daughters and the ladies of the Tudor House. Yet these changes, though they meant that certain lay undergraduates received a University education, did not alter the fact that education was still under predominantly clerical direction. Nor did the Reformation bring any immediate change in this. Archbishop Laud, at one time President of St. John's College, Oxford, was as firm a believer in clerical control of University education as any pre-Reformation ecclesiastic.

The sixteenth century brought another important change in English University education. This educational system had been unique to England in that, while every other country of Europe fostered Universities in all the leading towns and even little Scotland maintained four Universities, England alone, over the centuries, contented itself with two—Oxford and Cambridge—and these two developed, in the sixteenth century, highly peculiar constitutions. In the Middle Ages, in Oxford and Cambridge, as elsewhere, the University was the administrative unit, the Colleges or Halls little more than lodging houses where under-graduates could abide while they were doing their University courses. In Oxford and Cambridge alone, a collegiate system far stronger than at any other University was developed—so much so that when in early post-Reformation years a visitor asked 'Where is the University of Oxford?' it was possible to reply with only slight exaggeration, 'There is no University of Oxford.' It was the College to which the under-graduate belonged. It was the College which controlled his entrance and his exit—which admitted him and, if necessary, expelled him, and the University was in many ways little more than a federation of Colleges. Lectures were not offered to all comers but reserved for members of the lecturer's college or of a few colleges. Had the inquirer asked the same question about Cambridge he would have received much the same answer. It has always been a custom of tea-table gossip to pretend that Oxford and Cambridge are very different places and the differences between them of most fundamental importance. It is true that in the English habit they jealously preserve and boast of certain differences of nomenclature. The Quadrangle at Oxford is a Court at Cambridge, the scout a gyp, the tutor a supervisor; but in reality the systems are very much the same—they are infinitely more like one another than either is like any other University anywhere in the world.

Even at its most extreme it would not be quite true to say that either University was a mere federation of Colleges. The degree which the undergraduate received at the conclusion of his course was, of course, a degree of the University—not of the College. Parliament imposed certain tests—mainly of a religious nature—for the admission to mem-bership, to degrees or to academic posts. Oxford and Cambridge were the only two non-territorial constituencies which returned members to Parliament. The Head of one or other of the Colleges in turn presided over the University for a year as Vice-Chancellor and he had very con-siderable disciplinary powers for any offences committed outside the College.

Oxford of the seventeenth or eighteenth or even the nineteenth century was a very different place from the Oxford of today. There were, it is true, town and gown and disputes and battles between them, as we see in Thomas Hughes' *Tom Brown at Oxford* or Rowlandson or *Verdant Green*. These were frequent and fierce enough but there was not at these earlier dates nor indeed until very recently any Oxford that was quite unconnected with the University. The general population con-sisted entirely of servants, innkeepers, shopkeepers and the like who ministered to the University's needs. There were in those days, of course, no Cowley motor works. Turner's picture shows how Oxford began at Magdalen Bridge and there were no houses along the Iffley Road. There was no North Oxford. 'Oxford', as Dean Church said, 'was at that time, as it were a Greek or Italian city state, living out its life quite divorced from what might be going on in London or elsewhere.' Oxford was entirely a University town, under the control of the University authorities. Dr Routh the centenarian President of Magdalen who became President in 1784 and only died in 1854 used to entertain his guests by reciting to them his memories, as a young Don, of undergraduates whom, at the sentence of the Vice-Chancellor, he had seen hanged at Gownsmen's Gallows near the present Holywell. When towards the end of the nineteenth century the internal combustion engine came in Lord Queensberry applied to the police for a licence to entitle him to shoot any motor bicyclist who travelled at more than twenty miles an hour.

The great revolution of 1688 brought a most curious change into Oxford life. The University had up till then been a genuinely religious corporation. No one disputed—least of all those who opposed him—the sincerity of Archbishop Laud's religious ambitions. Oxford was a religious—an Anglican—corporation and, with Charles I for a number of years establishing his headquarters there, it was also a Tory corporation. Thus it was, of course, antipathetic to Cromwell, and his changes were never popular at Oxford and with Charles II's accession things reverted to an older pattern, but with a difference. The Oxford authorities were still Anglican and still Tory, but the depth of their faith was now open to question. Some were to prove their sincerity by becoming non-jurors at the deposition of James II. Others were time-servers.

The Hanoverian succession naturally had no wish that Oxford should remain a place of Tory propaganda. On the other hand Walpole's policy was a policy of *quieta non movere*. He had no wish to fire the young aristocrats of the eighteenth century with any missionary enthusiasm. Dean Jackson of Christ Church, the leading Head of a College of that century, had, records George Cox the Beadle of the University, in his *Recollections*, 'a wonderful tact in managing that most ungovernable class of undergraduates, noblemen'. It did not greatly matter if the young men learnt nothing so long as they did not learn Tory or Jacobite principles. It was Burnet, the Bishop of Salisbury, panegyrist of William III and author of the *Bishop Burnet's History of His Own Time*, who first conceived the idea that if the new regime was to be secure, it was necessary to take steps in order to make sure that the youth were not imbued with contrary principles at their Universities. Townshend, Walpole's brother-in-law, and Gibson, the Bishop of London, arranged that 'twenty-four persons who are Fellows of Colleges in the two Universities, twelve from Oxford and twelve from Cambridge, should preach an anti-Tory sermon each year at Whitehall'. For that sermon the preacher was to receive £30 and 'none must look for a share of that bounty but they who are staunch Whigs and declare themselves to be so'. It was a beginning, but it was not the habit of eighteenth-century courtiers to pay sufficient attention to sermons for it to be very likely that such would convert them to desirable political principles. It was necessary actually to invade the seats of education. 'No encouragement has hitherto been made', it was explained to King George I, 'at either of the said Universities for the study of modern history or modern languages and there has been opportunity frequently lost to the Crown of employing and encouraging members of the two Universities by conferring on them such employment both at home and abroad.' It was decided to create a number of Regius Professors with salaries of £400 a year and paying £25 to assistant teachers. These Professors were to deliver one lecture a term and 'to keep an eye on twenty scholars nominated by the King to be taught gratis' and every year 'to send an attested account of the progress made by each scholar to our principal Secretary of State'.

The consequence of this experiment was peculiar. It did not mean in the temper of the eighteenth century that enthusiastic propagandists should imbue their eager pupils with principles of Whiggish and Protestant history. On the contrary we discover that the Professors very soon came to treat their posts as sinecures. 'When I first read my warrant,' said Professor Nares, who was appointed to one of these Professorships, 'I well remember feeling ashamed of my ignorance of this curious science' (political economy) but, arrived at Oxford, he found his colleagues indifferent and as ignorant as he himself and 'the young men too constantly engaged upon higher pursuits' to attend to 'a subject comparatively so light and unacademical as modern history'. Pocketing his salary he retired to his house in Surrey, reflecting that 'if the office was to be bestowed on some resident member of the University things might be better'.

It is not very clear what these higher pursuits may have been. We have the evidence of, for instance, Gibbon's *Autobiography* as to the life of an undergraduate in the eighteenth century. It was, it will be remembered, almost uniquely unacademical, 'a place of learned torpor'. Adam

Smith said they 'had given up altogether even the pretence of learning'. Some half-century before Gibbon, Dudley Ryder had in 1713 painted very much the same picture. 'The best part of our conversation was concerning the University of Oxford. As for the public lectures, he says nobody regards them, they are all looked upon as mere useless things and rather for form's sake than for any profit the students gain by them, and as for the private lectures by the tutors they are very little more profitable. . . . So that they seem indeed to have no advantage for study there over any other place and the young men go there rather for the sake of its having been said that they have been at the University than for any advantages to improve them in knowledge.'

Up till the end of the eighteenth century in order to get a degree it was not necessary to pass any examination. All that was necessary was to remain at Oxford for the prescribed number of terms and to avoid being hanged. The instruction, such as it was, was entirely in Latin and Greek. It was not necessary to believe in the established religion or to practise meticulously its morals. All that was required was to profess belief by signing the Thirty-Nine Articles and to give such evidence of belief as was furnished by attending at Chapel and receiving the statutory number of times the Anglican Sacrament. The spirit in which in the early years of the nineteenth century the undergraduates at Trinity received the Sacrament—how it was then the custom to emerge from the Chapel in order to get drunk—will be remembered from the earlier passages of Newman's *Apologia*, and there is no reason at all to think that the undergraduates of Trinity were in this respect any different from the undergraduates of other Colleges. 'I consider the sending of a son thither' (i.e. to Oxford) wrote the headmaster of Tonbridge, 'without particular precautions a measure which may probably make shipwreck of his learning, his morals, his health, his character and his future.'

Of course, this subordination of the Church so that it became little more than a police department of State, was also to be found in every country of Europe, Catholic or Protestant. But the prevailing formula of *cuius regio eius religio*, by which the Treaty of Westphalia settled the century-long battle between the Catholics and the Protestants, did not mean that in eighteenth-century England or in eighteenth-century Oxford religion was entirely extinguished. The century, after all, saw John Wesley at Lincoln and Samuel Johnson at Pembroke, but in general the Church of England was thought of, not as a guardian of Christian truth, but as the defender of the existing order and of the rights of property. What genuine religious feeling is there in the clergy-men of Jane Austen?

Every College at Oxford had its Fellows who obtained their fellow-ships for the most part not through any evidence of academic merit but through sinecure privileges, which attached a fellowship to certain localities for which the benefactor had bequeathed the money. New Fellows were in general appointed by existing Fellows for reasons of favouritism. They were with few exceptions in Anglican orders. The belief that a clergyman should necessarily be celibate had of course been repudiated at the Reformation. But by a most curious chance this rule of celibacy was still imposed upon Fellows of Colleges. The Head of the College alone was permitted a wife. Only a very few of the Fellows undertook tutorial work. The great majority of them had no duties of any sort and made little pretence of scholarship. Boswell asked Johnson whether it was not an evil that so few of the Fellows should undertake any tutorial work but Johnson would have none of this. 'No, sir,' he said, 'a College would not get more advantage from having more than one or two of those pupil-mongers. If a boy has a hunger for learning he will do well enough; if he wants it he will not profit greatly from the best tutor.' As Mr Green's *Oxford Common Room* shows, they sat about drinking port and betting one another on such topics as which of com-peting cockroaches would succeed in crossing the Common Room to the opposite wall most rapidly, until eventually the needs of nature compelled them to the refuge of matrimony and they exchanged their fellowships for a College living. 'Jerusalem be damned. Give us wine, women and horses,' exclaimed a clerical Fellow of St John's, when Dean Stanley offered to speak in the Common Room about Jerusalem from which he had recently returned.

The Church had been regarded as the defender of the existing order and the *status quo* in the eighteenth century. The attacks of the French Revolution in the opinion of most Churchmen increased the importance of this function, and to them this was its almost exclusive function, in the early years of the nineteenth century. Ecclesiastics fought desperately in every ditch to protect their privileges—opposed Catholic Emancipa-tion, the Repeal of the Test Acts and of course the removal of Jewish disabilities—would admit no mitigation of the obligation for under-graduates or the recipients of degrees to subscribe the Thirty-Nine Articles. There was, in general, little revival in those early years, of any genuine religious fervour or of the feeling that religious profession involved any obligation to practise Christian morals. The more general feeling was of agreement with Lord Melbourne that 'I have the greatest respect for the Church of England, but things have come to a pretty pass if a man's religious professions are expected to interfere with his private life.' Lord Palmerston was one of the members for Cambridge University. His clerical constituents raised no objection at all to his flagrantly immoral private life, but thought seriously of depriving him of his seat when he supported Catholic Emancipation.

To the politicians, not careful of their personal morality or of their personal beliefs, the Church of England at the beginning of the nineteenth century at Oxford was defended in this spirit by those numerous clerical Fellows, the two bottle men, whom the Tractarians satirised as the 'Z's' —the nickname they gave to those of the lowest churchmanship. Cobbett attacked them as tithe-engrossers, stealers of Abbey lands and pilferers of enclosures. But there were Anglicans who came to see that the Church could never be an effective defender of the established order if it stood on grounds that were purely cynical, the more so if the cynicism of its defenders was unconscious, as it so largely was. On such a battleground it must in the end lose to the braver Methodists. Therefore there arose within the Church movements to revivify it—first the Evangelical movement, which sought to recall the faithful to the precepts of the Gospel and to enlist their support for such consequent causes as the abolition of the slave trade, and later the so-called Oxford movement, which proclaimed the essential membership of the Church of England as a branch of the Catholic Church and the validity of their orders and Sacraments. It is no part of this work to trace out the precise tenets of either of these movements. Our concern is rather with their effect and with the effect of the residual secularism of the Z's on the undergraduate life of the day.

It can be exaggerated. If we look to Newman's *Loss and Gain* we might get the impression that the main topic of undergraduate conversation in the 1830's was whether it was or was not right to take the step into the Church of Rome. If we read about the debates in Congregation concerning the condemnation of Ward's *Ideal of a Christian Church* we get the impression of intense undergraduate excitement about these ideas. The undergraduates turned out, booed the Vice-Chancellor, cheered Ward, threw their snowballs. But it would be certainly an error to interpret their ebullience entirely as an interest in the high intrinsic theological issues. To a large extent they booed the Vice-Chancellor and threw their snowballs as undergraduates do, out of mere high spirits. The number of the crowd who were acquainted with the subtle points at issue was small. One has only to turn to Newman's account of his Trinity under-graduate contemporaries—admittedly a few years earlier—for confirmation. We find that they accepted without question the restrictive rules of the College—signed the Thirty-Nine Articles and took the Sacraments as they were instructed—but that it never occurred to them to take such exercises seriously or to refrain from getting drunk as soon as the Sacrament was consumed—not even though a very considerable proportion of them were looking forward to taking Holy Orders in a few years' time. We get much the same picture from Thackeray's *Pendennis* —undergraduates to whom it does not occur to question the rules that confine the privileges of the University to those who would sign the Thirty-Nine Articles, who do not at all complain of the discipline of compulsory chapel but in whose conversations religious matters play no predominant part one way or the other. Or turn to *Tom Brown at Oxford*, the companion volume of the famous *Tom Brown's Schooldays*. The author of this was of course Thomas Hughes, pupil of the famous Dr Arnold of Rugby, who was a well-known Broad Churchman, and in the book we get a picture of an undergraduate society not much concerned with the niceties of theology or with schools of churchmanship, in which Puseyism and Grey, its ineffectual chaplain, play a passing role, but a society intensely concerned with broad moral principles which were considered to be based upon a religious foundation.

With the end of the eighteenth century the purely formal examination for degrees of previous years was modified. Fellowships which up till then had only been open to examination at certain Colleges such as Oriel were made more generally the reward of merit and ability, and honours for final examinations were instituted. Yet even then only a small proportion of undergraduates read for honours. The great majority of the undergraduates were still content with a pass degree. Commoners were, of course, admitted to the University but they were second-class under-graduates—inferior to the aristocrats who had special gowns and ate their dinners in Hall at separate tables. Their interests naturally were not often in theology. The Church to them, if it received any respect at all, was respected merely as a convenient conservative institution. A few poor boys, servitors, were admitted to Oxford education on con-dition that they served as fags for their betters.

In 1851 Sir William Hamilton wrote a stinging attack on the Univer-sity of Oxford as it then was. In it he recorded—perhaps with exaggera-tion—'The University of Oxford is distinguished at once for the extent to which the most important interests of the public have been sacrificed to private advantage—for the unhallowed disregard in its accomplishments of every moral and religious bond—for the sacred character of the agents through which the unholy treason was perpetrated—for the systematic perjury it has nationalised in this great seminary for religious education—for the apathy with which the injustice has been tolerated by the State, the impiety by the Church—nay, even for the unacquaintance so manifested by so flagrant a corruption.' Oxford was of all academical institutions the most imperfect and the most perfectible. . . . On the average there is to be found among those to whom Oxford confides the business of education an infinitely smaller proportion of men of literary reputation than among the actual instructors of any other University in the world. The causes of decay were the religious tests for entry and the disproportion by which the Colleges which ought to have been merely lodging houses had been allowed to grow at the expense of the University into self-governing schools.

The years 1851 and 1871—the years of the appointment of a Royal Commission on the Universities and of the final abolition of all religious tests—are the watershed years in Oxford's nineteenth-century history. They cannot be better traced than through a study of that strange and enigmatic character—Mark Pattison. Mark Pattison had at the time of the launching of the Oxford Movement been a fervent Puseyite and admirer of Newman. In his later years, though still remaining in Holy Orders and from time to time under some protest conducting Anglican services, he became a strong anti-clerical and more or less an unbeliever. He was critical of compulsory chapel in contrast to Walter Pater at Brasenose who was its strong defender. With the tergiversations of his character, his almost insanely melancholic father, his differences with his wife, his quarrels with the Fellows of Lincoln over whom as Rector he had to preside, we are not here concerned. Our concern is with the picture that he leaves to us of the undergraduates of the day. In the first half of the century he was a keen reformer, demanding the abolition of abuses and of clerical privileges. In those years he established very close relations with his undergraduate pupils—much closer than was then the general custom—and was much admired by them. In his closing years he developed the thesis, which he had derived from Germany, that the essential business of a University was to foster works of learned scholarship. He quarrelled with Jowett's belief that a University should be a continuation of a public school or that Dons' first business was with their pupils. In spite of their wide differences in his closing years Pattison remained to the end an admiring friend of Newman. Yet it is interesting to compare his ambition for a University with that of Newman in his *Idea of a University*, which is solely concerned with the training of undergraduates and pays no attention at all to the need for producing scholars of research.

Morose habits grew upon Pattison and he displayed them both to his pupils and to most other people. 'A large minority of the young men who matriculate', he wrote, 'are not only entirely unfit to satisfy the requirements of the place but are in a state which renders it almost hopeless to expect that they will ever be fit to do so.' The proportion of undergraduates who read for honours, though increasing, was still small. The pass men, poll men, he thought, had no business at the University at all. Yet it was, he thought, even less likely that one would get this appreciation of the true purpose of a University from the British elec- torate than from the unreformed Fellows. So he waned in his enthusiasm for reform. On the other hand he strongly supported means for reducing the cost of an Oxford course, advocating for instance that the poor should be allowed to lodge in Halls rather than in the more expensive Colleges. He supported the abolition of privileges for noblemen, he criticised the habits of entertainment and the time and money spent on organised games such as cricket.

It was not of course by any means all of his fellow Heads of Colleges who sympathised with his ambition to make a University education available to men of all means. The snub which the Master of Biblioll College, as Thomas Hardy calls it, dealt out to Jude the Obscure when Jude revealed to him his ambition to become an undergraduate will be remembered. Cardinal College in the novel was Christ Church and Pattison was always at especially bitter war with Christ Church which he looked upon as the high warden of useless snobbery.

The result of the reforms of 1871 were of course considerable. A Jew, Professor Alexander the philosopher, was elected a Fellow, the first of his faith. Catholics in small numbers began to come to the University and did not come in larger numbers only because of the opposition to their going there of the Catholic authorities. The Colleges still certainly belonged to the Fellows and the gap between them and the under- graduates was large but it was less than it had been. The gap between the Head of a College and the other Fellows was still considerable. There was still no retiring age for University appointments; McGrath remained Provost of Queen's until his death in his nineties and in the early years of this century, spending his last twenty years in bed and paying £50 a year to his Vice-Provost for doing his duties. Clerical tests were of course then abolished and over the years agnosticism has certainly been more common among the Fellows than among their pupils. When Pattison arrived in Oxford he found the scholars among the under-graduates were despised as a sort of servitor. The aristocrats were then called tufts. The word derived from the tufted patch or tuft found on top of the hair in some birds. It was applied to the gold tassels worn on their caps by undergraduates of noble birth since 1670 and became a general nickname for noble undergraduates in 1775. They were excused all examinations, and were immensely more regarded by the Dons. Pattison lived to see the scholars considered as persons to be respected.

It is the English way that such changes manifest themselves in the long run but not immediately. Just as after 1832 the type of man who was returned to the House of Commons did not immediately change so very much but over the course of years the middle-class manufacturer was able to challenge the predominance of the landed gentleman, so at Oxford in spite of the abolition of clerical privileges the worst fears of Pusey were not realised and for some years Fellows with clerical collars were still the majority at High Tables, even though it might perhaps be questionable what secret beliefs lay behind those collars.

Though Pattison, the Rector, was a strong anti-clerical and though after the removal of the tests the Fellows no longer had to be in Holy Orders, nevertheless in the closing years of Pattison's life a third of the undergraduates at Lincoln were the sons of clergymen—and no doubt the proportion was similar at other Colleges. Of these sons of the clergy a good proportion went on to be clergymen themselves. All the Colleges still maintained their chapels and a chaplain-Fellow to minister to them. Yet the faith of the chaplains was becoming steadily more modernist, the chapels less well attended, compulsory attendance at some of them less insisted on and, of course, the requirement of Communion as a test for membership quite abandoned as an indecency. Instead of attending chapel in the morning, undergraduates at some Colleges were allowed to present themselves by a certain hour in Hall and have their names checked off. Dress was becoming steadily less formal. Gladstone, who combined the most rigidly conservative habits with his liberal opinions, complained that the undergraduates of his old age were much less formally and tidily dressed than had been those of his youth. One trembles to think what would have been his verdict on the under-graduates of today!

In the years before the First War Christ Church still kept that social superiority among Colleges for which Pattison had so strongly attacked it. Wykehamists still went to New College. Oriel had for a time had the most distinguished Senior Common Room. It had never had any marked superiority in undergraduates. Its prestige had declined a little. The superiority among undergraduates in the years up to the war certainly rested with Balliol. Jowett, though himself in orders, had adopted completely the new secularist spirit of the age. 'A priest is a more important person than a judge,' someone once said to him, 'for a judge can only say "You be hanged" but a priest can say "You be damned."' 'Yes, but if a judge says "You be hanged",' replied Jowett, 'you are hanged.' In every age, he thought, the ablest people have always been ministers of the established religion, 'but they have always disbelieved in it'. Jowett accepted with enthusiasm the secular programme of the abolition of ecclesiastical privileges. His ambition, in which he largely succeeded, was to collect a College of undergraduates from all walks of society: a few black men; a few members of the lower classes; some Scotsmen; a Catholic or two, like Hilaire Belloc; and to train up those who were afterwards to be the governors of the nation. Pattison, as has been seen, was bitterly contemptuous of this ambition to turn a University career into a prolongation of public school days. Sligger Urquhart, the Catholic Dean of Balliol (he was known as Sligger, he once told me, because in his youth he was supposed to be very sleek, and the sligger was a corruption of the sleeker), wrote in 1905, 'My idea is that we should get the best men (in several ways) from our public schools and let them mix with intelligent men from Birmingham, etc. That will be best for both sets. At present we seem to have too many of the latter. The result is that they don't mix, partly because they can form a world of their own, partly because the public schoolboys feel them-selves rather in a minority and crowd together and because they have not enough grown-up interests to link them to the others.' Urquhart, a man of many virtues and much piety, was certainly a snob and, for himself, greatly preferred the company of the public school men to those from 'Birmingham, etc.' He held open house in the evening for those from the more famous schools and when someone who had not such advantages intruded upon him he received short shrift. 'What book have you come to borrow, Thompson?' he was asked and summarily ushered out again from the room, offered no refreshment. But, whatever the cause of the attempts of Jowett and his successors to mix classes in a society which was still profoundly class-divided, the success was im-perfect. Balliol's black men were of course a legend and were much derided by their racially pure neighbours in Trinity. Yet, blacks apart, racialism in Balliol was rampant. Old Etonians drove Sir Philip Sassoon out of Balliol Quad with horse whips.

> The things that a fellow don't do,
> The things that a fellow don't do.
> They have not been told to the Board school boy
> They have not been revealed to the Jew

they sang against the outcasts. Aristocratic undergraduates like Charles Lister professed to be socialists but socially the public schoolboys kept to themselves and did not much mix with 'Birmingham, etc.' Very often Etonians even did not mix much with those from other and despised public schools. Drink was cheap and drunkenness fairly frequent and not much considered. Charles Lister was sent down for insulting the Dean of Trinity in his cups. 'I wist not that it was the High Priest', Ronald Knox inscribed on a stone to commemorate his misfortune and mock funeral. Those of that day differed, it seems, from the undergraduates of the 1920's in the quite inordinate amount of time that they spent in debating clubs and in pseudo-intellectual societies for reading one anothers papers.

The main differences between undergraduate life in those years and that of the 1920's was the absence of buses; Cowley and Morris had not yet come into existence. I remember the Oxford of those earlier years, though not as an undergraduate; I was a preparatory schoolboy at Summer Fields up the Banbury Road. Oxford was then still served by horse trams, which Oscar Wilde in his day had denounced as an odious modernism. Gerard Manley Hopkins described Oxford of those years as

> having a base and brickish skirt . . .
> Towery city and branchy between towers;
> Cuckoo-echoing, bell-swarmèd, lark-charmèd, rook-racked,
> river-rounded.

I remember how in 1913 the young bicycle-mender Mr Morris, put the motor buses on the roads in competition against the horse trams. Everyone said that they could not possibly succeed. No Oxford man could be expected to ride in a motor bus when he had the chance of riding in a horse tram. In fact, of course, as we know, the horse trams were beaten and the old tram-lines removed. After the war old soldiers who had been up at Oxford before the war used to come back to visit their old University. They would be discovered late at night in their cups hopelessly searching the streets for the now non-existent tram-lines which they vaguely remembered as the only sure route which might carry them back to their Colleges. Homosexuality was before the war much less freely discussed. There is no overt mention in any pre-war reminiscences of homosexual attractions and even less of homosexual practices. Yet it is well known that such practices were a great problem in public schools at that period, not allowed by the authorities to be in any way an expression of romance and condemned as the sin crying to heaven for vengeance and punished on discovery by instant expulsion. In that the spirit of the late Victorians was far different from that of the earlier years of the nineteenth century.

Women ('does' as it was the fashion to call them) were not allowed to play any part in the general social life of pre-war Oxford. They only appeared at Eights Week or in the confessedly fantastic pages of *Charley's Aunt* or of *Zuleika Dobson*. In the Oxford of the 1920's homosexuality was freely discussed among undergraduates. It is not to be believed that such affections were not known, even if they were not freely talked about, in pre-war Oxford. The activities of the Bloomsburyites from Cambridge (the Higher Sodomy, as they were called) at the same time, are today common knowledge but they were not at that time so freely published. It is fairly obvious that in *Sinister Street*, Michael Fane, who was very outspoken in his pronouncements that, unlike his creator Compton Mackenzie, he would have nothing to do with women and at the same time deeply romantic in his general view of life was a man who at this period of his life at any rate was prone to homosexual affections. Reticence about these affections was perhaps the main difference between pre-war Oxford and the Oxford of the 1920's.

The other College beside Balliol of whose life in these pre-war days we have the fullest record is Magdalen. This is partly because of the popularity of *Sinister Street* in which Magdalen is depicted as St Mary's and partly because it was the College in which, as a result of the ultra-snobbish intrigues of its President, Sir Herbert Warren, the Prince of Wales (afterwards Edward VIII) was in those years an undergraduate and partly because it was the College of Oscar Wilde and Lord Alfred Douglas. It had been the College of Routh, the famous centenarian. Raymond Asquith in his inimitable satiric poem 'Lines on a Young Viscount Who Died on the Morrow of a Bump Supper' portrays Sir Herbert Warren as saying:

Yet we who know the larger Love
Which separates the sheep and goats,
And segregates Scolecobrotes,
Believing where we cannot prove,

Deem that in his mysterious way
God puts the Peers upon his right
And hides the poor in endless night,
For thou, my Lord, art more than they.

Anthony Wood, defying the verdict on Wadham quoted on a subsequent page of this book, called Magdalen 'the most noble and rich structure in the learned world'. It was then, though it has since become less so, an aristocratic College in the sense that a large number of its undergraduates were from the most fashionable schools. They expressed their College spirit in a rousing chorus, which is, I am told, now quite forgotten.

Let the spirit of the past
Like a mantle round us cast,
    Be our heritage and glory cast before us
And we'll raise and raise again
The victorious refrain
    Of Magdalena Floreat in chorus

Less attention was there paid to degrees in final schools than at Balliol. There was no pressure on men to read for honours if they preferred a pass degree. Magdalen men were much less prominent than Balliol men at the Union. Indeed it was their fashion to despise that society. They spent less time in attending societies, debating with one another or reading one anothers papers, more time in dinners and semi-formal after-dinner drinking parties. As at Balliol, there were undergraduates who had not been at important schools, but the public school men treated these with offensive brutality. In *Sinister Street* it was only the influence of the admirable buttery-keeper, Venner, which prevented the public school men from violently attacking the plebeian Smithers for no reason other than his undistinguished origin. Again, as with Charles Lister at Balliol, some of the public school men were willing to air theoretically egalitarian opinions but there was no serious suggestion that the undergraduate from the town grammar school would in practice ever challenge the public school predominance of Oxford society. A much more common topic of conversation than this threat both among Dons and among undergraduates of the upper classes at Magdalen was whether the coming of the Rhodes scholars would prove a menace to Oxford's social life. There is no mention of any black men at St Mary's.

When Michael Fane was asked to lunch by a man at Lincoln he pretended ignorance of where that College was. 'I don't know where Lincoln is. Have you got a map or something of Oxford?' he asked. The Compton Mackenzie of history tells us in Octave Three of *My Life and Times* how when Magdalen had to play Keble in a football match he hired a coach and four to take him to the match, believing or pretending to believe that Keble lay somewhere out in the country. Michael Fane told Guy Hazlewood that at St Mary's the undergraduates were younger and the Dons older than at other Colleges. Guy answered that at Balliol it was just the other way round.

So much for Oxford before 1914. The following six chapters are concerned with Oxford after the First War. They make no attempt at a detailed, statistical description of the University during those years. I have rather given sketches of five men who were undergraduates at that time, whom I happened to know intimately. They were all, I fancy, interesting men and all have left their mark on the life of England, a mark which first began to show itself at Oxford. I do not pretend that all undergraduates of those years resembled them. They were all indeed not only notable but also eccentric, but nevertheless I do not consider it exaggerated to think that between them they in their different ways were reasonably representative of the Oxford of their years.

# Maurice Bowra

Settled *Hoti's* Business
*A Grammarian's Funeral*—Robert Browning

Oxford reassembled after the war. The Dons were for the moment of course all Dons of the pre-war vintage, returning as the case might be, from military service or from their desks in government departments. Of the undergraduates some came, as in pre-war days, direct from school, a greater number in the first years after the war from military service. Of those whose Oxford life had been interrupted by the war some, like, for instance, Mr Harold Macmillan, did not care to take it up again and forwent the degree. Others went up and found, after the interruption of the trenches, a difficulty in applying themselves to Latin and Greek but thought it worthwhile, in order to qualify for future appointments, to scramble through the shortened course which the University offered and to equip themselves with the degree as rapidly as possible. Military life was still the life which they thought of as normal and they referred to Hall as the Mess. To others the Oxford life was a blessed relief after the horrors of the trenches and they entered into it with all gusto and delight. Of no one was this more true than of Maurice Bowra, who was an undergraduate of New College, immediately after the war and went on from that to be Fellow and then Dean and Warden of Wadham, Proctor and Vice-Chancellor, the most competent administrator of Oxford's affairs and by general consent the leading figure in the University's inter-war years.

Maurice Bowra was the son of Cecil Bowra, administrator of the Chinese Customs, and was born and, in his early years, brought up in China. He was sent home for school, as was then the custom, and went to Cheltenham, where his career was reasonably, but not exceptionally, distinguished. He took little interest in the ordinary school activities or its games. We used afterwards at Oxford sometimes to play tennis together, but a game was to him always an essentially comic activity to be accompanied with ribald laughter and on no account to be taken seriously. Though he read widely at school he did not confine his reading to any set curriculum. In after years he was always critical of the rigidity of Cheltenham as of most other public schools. He was amused once when visiting the school to be told by one of the masters that in that master's opinion instructions for Confirmation were overdone, so much so that 'on the day boys were delivered stale at the post'. When Maurice was at the school and up to August, 1914, Houston Stewart Chamberlain, the great apostle of German racialism, was honoured as one of the school's most distinguished old boys. After that, to Maurice's amusement, his name was discreetly removed from the roll. Yet ironic as he was, behind his irony Maurice always kept a friendship with his old school headmaster, Dr Butterfield, and used to go and stay with him at Hereford where he had retired as Dean. He was pleased to be asked to accept, and accepted, membership of the Governing Body of the school.

Just before the war he had won a scholarship at New College, Oxford and would in the ordinary course, had not the war come, have gone up in the next October. Instead he joined the Royal Field Artillery and served in the trenches in France. The experience left him with an abiding loathing of war and contempt for the military minds who mismanaged it. He hated it so much that in after life he did not often care to talk about it and Mr Anthony Powell records how in passing by Gallipoli on a Hellenic cruise he had to go below and lie down in his cabin for half an hour. 'Whatever you hear about the war,' he later told Cyril Connolly who had of course been too young to share in it, 'remember it was far worse—worse—inconceivably bloody—nobody who wasn't there can ever imagine what it was like.' His reaction to it was not unlike that of Siegfried Sassoon. The war, he came to think, was an obscene act of insanity. The early hysterical mood of denunciation of Belgian atrocities was long past before it was his time to go to France. He thought and saw no evil in the Germans, who to his mind were no different from and no worse than the English or anyone else. On the other hand it never occurred to him to be a pacifist or conscientious objector. The war was just a horror and an obscenity which had been sent to us. There was no alternative but to accept it and endure it.

Demobilised from the army, he came up to New College in 1919. I arrived a year later in October 1920, and we soon heard of his reputation throughout the University as the leading wit among the resident undergraduates. He had just got a brilliant First in his Mods, receiving, we were told, a record number of Alphas in his papers. We took the brilliance of his success for granted. But success in the examination by itself would not have won him any special reputation. There were brilliantly successful examinees who lived in their secluded rooms with 'oaks' sported at the tops of towers and who never emerged into the light of day. Enoch Powell is said to have later lived such a life at Cambridge. To us Oxford was primarily a place of social adventure and it was for the brilliance of the social circle which he led that we heard of Maurice Bowra. He was at New College and I at Balliol, but he never confined himself to members of his own college. He had friends at Balliol—in particular Leslie Hartley, then a very harmless and necessary cat, who lingered on at Oxford writing prize essay after prize essay, patronising his juniors with infinite kindness but showing signs of becoming what we know among Americans as a permanent undergraduate, afterwards of course to blossom out into one of our leading novelists, and it was, I think, through him that I first got to know Maurice Bowra. I was noticed and flattered to be noticed. I was invited to one of the large luncheons which it was then possible for undergraduates to offer in their rooms in College and which he most delighted to give. I knew little then of his precise opinions, but got an inkling of them when I chanced to make a remark of the unpopularity which, so I had somewhere read, the early Christians had earned among butchers in Bithynia owing to the reduced consumption of meat which was a consequence of their asceticism. Keynes had then just published his book and it was of course on all educated tongues. 'Economic Consequences of the Christ,' said Bowra, and I gained from the general titter that here was a circle in which it was fashionable to make gentle fun of religion. At that time it was the fashion to call a man with a beard a beaver, and Maurice recited with amusement and approval Aldous Huxley's quatrain about such a man.

> Of decorous behaviour,
> He was a true believer.
> He'd imitate Our Saviour
> And cultivate a beaver.

Though he had friends outside College, yet it was with men from New College and particularly with members of New College Essay Society that he principally consorted. The New College Essay Society was a society of bright undergraduates who met together in one another's rooms on a Saturday evening, when the host read an essay on some topic not concerned with the school that he was reading. It was the custom to enliven the paper with epigrams and witticisms, or pretended witticisms, according to the fashion of the day and the talent of the reader. The paper was followed by the drinking of a loving cup and by a discussion, in which the critic stood in front of the fire and delivered himself of his criticisms on the paper of the evening. Of the papers delivered at that time that which aroused the greatest interest was Jack Haldane's *Daedalus*—a scientific prophecy of the future of the world. It was published and was at the time much talked about.

Among Bowra's main cronies at that time were Cyril Radcliffe, with whom he was afterwards to share digs opposite Oriel, today of course the well-known judge—Eric Strauss, the psychiatrist who was to cure Evelyn Waugh of his Pinfold troubles—Deane Jones, the son of a Nonconformist minister in Birmingham, who became a Don at Merton and died young—Roy Harrod, now Sir Roy Harrod, who became a Don at Christ Church and who reinforced Bowra's belief that the war of 1914 was an unnecessary folly—Amyas Ross, the son of a Somerset vicar who went to school at Repton and afterwards, for a time, became a Communist, then forsaking the Communist faith for the Douglas Credit Scheme and also dying young, and Hew Anderson of the shipping family who was himself an artist rather than a man of commerce. There were others less known today.

The mark of them was that they were all men of brilliance, who, unlike many other undergraduates of that and the immediately succeeding period, took their schools seriously and did well in them, but to whom it never occurred that the gaining of a degree could be the sole purpose of Oxford life. Conversation, whether at the Essay Society or over the cups or at the luncheon or dinner table was valued at least as highly. The conversation both among the intellectuals at New College and among those who regarded themselves as intellectuals at Balliol or other colleges was very much of the type of which undergraduate conversation has, I suppose, always consisted. 'Undergraduates,' as Warden Spooner truly said, 'recur'. True things were sometimes said. Undergraduates learnt very important lessons from their fellow undergraduates that they would never have learnt from a formal examination paper. Literature was much quoted and discussed. Pictures and artists played their part in arguments. There was talk about the problems and tribulations of the world. Religion and sex were on many unofficial agenda. There were no doubt circles in which music played its important part, but it happens that it did not bulk very large in Maurice Bowra's life.

Nor did science. Jack Haldane was the only member of this New College set who made any scientific pretensions and he, though he taught science, had no scientific degree.

It cannot be denied that witty epigram was sometimes preferred to deeper truth or that to raise a laugh even those who were at heart kindly and genial at times did not forbear to say wounding things about their fellows. In private parties they indulged in an amusing game by which one of the players wrote some lines of verse, then covered over all but the last line which he handed to his neighbour so that he might add a final line to rhyme with the line that he had been shown but in ignorance of what had preceded it. They also enjoyed making Clerihews about the Roman Emperors such as:

> The Emperor Arcadius
> Lived outside the five mile radius,
> Which made it rather laborious
> To visit the Emperor Honorius

or:

> The Emperor Nero
> Was not a Christian hero.
> He used communicants
> As illuminants.

They composed cruder limericks such as one on Deane Jones:

> There once was a Fellow of Merton
> Who went down the street with no shirt on.
> He would titivate shyly
> His membrum virile
> For the people to animadvert on.

Maurice and I had a rather offensive habit of reciting in very loud voices certain poems which we both knew by heart—particularly from Chesterton's *Wine, Water and Song*. It was not much fun for those who were not acquainted with the poem. I remember one such complaining, 'There are some sorts of talk that I just cannot do with.'

The New College coterie played another and less attractive game, by which all those present selected certain qualities and awarded marks for them to all the other members of the company. Some of the qualities were innocuous, but sometimes they voted on such defects as bad breath, sex attraction, ill-washed neck and the like—where low marks received from a friend were easily able to cause what Maurice called 'bad blood'. As Mr Anthony Powell writes of him, 'Everything about him was up to date. The innovation was not only to proclaim the paramount claims of eating, drinking and sex (if necessary, auto-erotic) but accepting as absolutely natural open snobbishness, success-worship, personal vendettas, unprovoked malice, disloyalty to friends, reading other people's letters (if not lying about to be sought in unlocked drawers)—the whole bag of tricks.' But I do not think that Mr Powell is quite fair. He does not allow enough for Maurice's high spirits. What he writes is true but not the whole truth.

He was never married. At one time he was engaged to a lady whom many of his friends thought to be not quite worthy of him. When asked why he had not made a better choice, he replied, 'Buggers can't be choosers.' He shared this defiance of convention with friends from Cambridge which gave rise to the verse:

> Oh, for the sofas of Sodom
> With their soft and voluptuous springs,
> If I were the Warden of Wadham
> And you were a Fellow of King's.

In his Foundation Oration at London University in 1967 he said, 'I am sure that this is the thing that the young value—that they know their own personalities, which are too serious to be badgered and pushed about by a lot of silly rules they do not agree with. . . . There the Twenties laid the foundation and we ought to be grateful to them.' This is a more fair description of his general outlook, even if the critic might be tempted to paraphrase it, 'How much we admire ourselves.'

For the older generation he had no hostility but in general little respect. I remember when Sir Henry Wilson was murdered that Maurice made a great parade of announcing that his murder was a good thing since he was a diplomat and 'soldiers who are good diplomats should always be murdered'. The young with him were confident that they knew best, or at any rate were confident that the old did not know, and it must be confessed that they could point to the formidable evidence of the 1914 war to prove as much. He praised Maurice Dick as 'the new kind of Don'. 'They give tutorials with a bottle of whisky by the arm-chair and a girl in the bedroom.'

Bowra never allowed himself to become involved in politics. He only once in his Oxford career spoke at the Union and that very many years after he had ceased to be an undergraduate. He never joined any of the political clubs or attended any of their dinners. Unlike many of the rest of us he never became involved with Frank Gray, who was in those days winning Oxford for the Liberals and whom, when he walked from Banbury to Oxford in a race in battle-kit, Evelyn Waugh in the *Cherwell* referred to in derision as 'Mr Gray, a Liberal politician'. He was, as were most of the bright young undergraduates of the day, politically, vaguely of the left. Nor was he much interested in those problems of University politics by which undergraduates, who are today often called students, are now so greatly occupied. There was then no demand for Students' Unions or for undergraduate self-government. Indeed it was difficult to get undergraduates to serve on J.C.R. Committees. I remember Sligger Urquhart complaining to me that whereas schoolboys were always anxious to become prefects, once they came up to the University they refused to take any positions of responsibility. The Proctors were wise enough to modify their regulations a little to meet the returning soldiers. Undergraduates were no longer required to wear but had to carry gowns at night, but were still required to be in College at twelve o'clock. I never remember even a conversation between undergraduates criticising the proctorial system. Certainly Maurice Bowra, himself in time to be a Proctor, was one of those who accepted the need for regulations without being very careful to obey them. Chapel was still theoretically compulsory at New College but Alic Smith, the Dean, made it clear that he would not enforce the regulation. H. A. L. Fisher, soon to be elected Warden, was confessedly an atheist.

The victory of the Coalition in the 1918 election had caused a great reaction against Conservative politics and against the 'hard-faced men who had done well out of the war'. Although he had not at this time made the friendship which he afterwards formed through Elizabeth Bibesco with the Asquith family, yet Maurice, he confesses in his autobiography, voted for an Asquithian Liberal—of course to no purpose— at the 1918 election. When I asked him early in our acquaintance what were his political opinions he replied, 'Anything except Coalition.' I remember one day at luncheon when asked to mention an important living writer, he sarcastically named Kipling amid titters of sycophantic laughter from his fellow lunchers. He came later to have a little more respect for the figures of the Establishment as indeed have many others. In fifty years, owing to the influence of T. S. Eliot, Auden, Kingsley Amis and others, the judgment of intellectuals on Kipling has very marvellously changed.

It never occurred to him at that time any more than it did to any of us that there was any possibility that we should ever in our lives see a second war. Yet he had a vague feeling that it was only right that, even if it was not so easily possible to make a land fit for heroes, it was at least important that a certain vengeance should be taken on the masters of the Establishment who had so misruled the land. Shortly before I came up there was a strike of the Oxford bus workers. Conventional Conservative undergraduates opposed the strikers, just as they were later in 1926 to oppose the workers who took part in the much more important General Strike. Progressives took the other side. Especially keen in the support of the strikers was Jack Haldane who imperilled his Fellowship by being caught one day emerging out of a manhole in a drain into the Oxford street. It is not quite clear why this escapade was in any way of advantage to the bus strikers but it was thought that it was conduct unbecoming to a Fellow of the College. Deane Jones who boarded a bus and threw off two blackleg bus conductors was equally unpopular. When the strike was all over a posse of *bienpensant* Conservative undergraduates invaded Deane Jones' room and threatened that they would destroy his furniture. His friends, including Maurice Bowra, rallied to his defence and a vigorous battle took place, which was only eventually concluded by the intervention of a near-by and inoffensive science Don reporting that the Warden requested that they should make less noise.

In general undergraduate liberalism of those days was of a curious sort. The majority of undergraduates were no doubt Conservatives but the majority of those who prided themselves on being intellectual or politically minded were Liberals, or at least of left opinions. But just as at Eton many of us had vaguely argued that it was only right that boys of poor parents should be admitted to the school but it had never occurred to any of us that, if places were found for such, there might be fewer places for the rest of us, so at Oxford after the 1914 war. Before the war there had been no general entrance examination beyond the formality of responsions for undergraduates. The condition for entrance was the ability to pay the fees. Yet the scholarship system provided a certain *carrière ouverte aux talents*. Poor boys could buy for themselves a University career by scholarships, and there was a sufficient variety of scholarships for a poor, able and very energetic boy to pay his whole way, making little or no demand on his parent's pocket. After the war egalitarian and liberal talk was more common on undergraduate lips than it had been before the war. Vague talk about homes for heroes had made such language familiar. On the other hand in fact the path of the poor boy to the University was more difficult than it had been before 1914.

The cost of living had risen, but the Colleges were not more affluent than they had been before the war and the scholarships which they offered were in no way increased in value. For the moment some demobilised soldiers were able to use their gratuities to buy themselves an education, In the closing months of the First War, when H. A. L. Fisher was President of the Board of Education, £8,000,000 was voted by Parliament to enable returning soldiers to pay for a University education, and 27,000 took advantage of the grant. But the principle of Government assistance of University education was criticised by many at Oxford, including the Vice-Chancellor of the day. That source was soon exhausted. Until the Asquith Commission reported, which had not yet happened at the date of which we are talking, rates and taxes made no contribution to undergraduates' education. It was more difficult to live on scholarships than it had been before the war and the number who did so was smaller.

The allowance which parents were able to give to their sons naturally varied from undergraduate to undergraduate. Some were kept in luxury, others hard pressed, but Bowra was better off than the majority, as were most of those with whom he consorted at the Essay Society. It is notable that, though they talked a great deal about the rights of the workers and though some of them even flirted with the ideas of Karl Marx, they were all in fact of public school origin and had very little to do with the working classes. Nor can it be pretended that Maurice Bowra ever very much consorted with the workers at any period of his life. He championed liberty. He genuinely disliked the stupid rich who made no contribution to the free society in exchange for their privileges, but the liberty which he valued was the liberty of the intellectual and the free exchange of ideas and his friends were almost entirely those who had traffic in such goods. A little later when I came up there was at the Union and elsewhere a good deal of rather absurd and ill-informed support of the Russian experiment and opposition to Winston Churchill's pleas for a war against the Bolsheviks, but those who indulged in such talk were careful to explain that they did so as the bulwarks and friends of freedom and not as Communists. There were at that time, I think, only two declared Communist Party members at the University, Mr Charles Grey and Mr Arthur Reid, and of these Mr Grey had been educated at Winchester and Bradfield and Mr Reid at Eton. They were both fairly well-to-do. Mr Grey announced with some pompous pride, 'I am a traitor to my class and proud of it', but that did not prevent him from keeping his private income.

It is noteworthy that none of Bowra's friends of the Essay Society ever afterwards went into Parliament, though Roy Harrod indeed in 1945 did stand for Huddersfield as a Liberal. I fancy that most of them, like him, voted Asquithian Liberal, even though they had not, like him, the additional impulse of friendship with the Asquith family to induce them to do so. They were anti-Conservative and, at any rate until the time of the Irish Treaty, there was little temptation for an anti-Conservative to attach himself to Lloyd George. I remember when Lloyd George came down to the Union and I, as an officer, had to attend the dinner beforehand, Maurice Bowra very kindly entertained to dinner my parents who happened at the time to be staying in Oxford and took them to the debate. He maintained—truly or falsely—that he once before had seen Lloyd George 'when he was running away at the time of the German attack on Good Friday of 1918'. Being anti-Conservative, he voted Liberal. But he was neither then nor indeed at any other time greatly interested in schemes for the organisation of society. 'Our civilisation', he was to write, 'is going to pot with books on Planning for God.' He and his friends had in general so little to do with the working classes that it was perhaps not surprising that genuine Trades Unionists from Ruskin College refused to take very seriously public school liberal undergraduates. Maurice Bowra's interest was in liberty and he did not find that that was a cause for which Trade Union Socialists very deeply cared. The liberties that he found threatened were mainly liberties of the intellectuals and the middle classes. A not unjust description of his true opinions were to be found in the satirical lines which he composed about New College's economics Don:

> The chief defect of Henry Clay
> Was clamouring for higher pay.
> By pandering to the working class
> He's brought us to a pretty pass.

Jack Haldane who was then a Communist, alone of his friends, I fancy, played an active part in what was then thought of as the battle of the proletariat. He used to go lecturing for the party throughout the Midland counties. Enthusiastic supporters gave him hospitality for the night, but he made his condition. He must be offered whisky after the lecture. 'I will not lecture on ovaltine,' he said in some disgust. In the same way Maurice and his friends gave theoretical support through their votes on appropriate occasions to the admission of women to the University, but they did not much consort with women or with women's colleges.

He was never very deeply interested in party politics. I remember that he complained to me that he could not understand them. 'I would have thought that if you believed something you should advocate it, but they tell me that is the very last thing you should do,' he once said to me. Naturally I knew more about conditions in Balliol, but I have no reason to think that they were much different at New College or anywhere else. We had our boys' club in Oxford down in the slums at St Old's but it was not much frequented—certainly not, I am ashamed to say, by me. With the 1920's the Government embarked on its policy of deflation, preparatory to going back to the gold standard. This involved a steady reduction of wages. Trade Union leaders were called upon to support such reductions. Miners refused but others consented. It was surprising how little undergraduates knew, or talked about such events. Our talk, in so far as it was concerned with politics, was much more concerned with reprisals in Ireland, of which as Liberals we generally disapproved.

Maurice Bowra hardly took any interest in working class movements until the General Strike of 1926 and even then his interest was only fitful and mainly inspired by his friendship with Hugh Gaitskell who was by then an undergraduate. My brother was at that time a Don at Hertford and I told Maurice how he had said, 'They tell me that it is a battle between the classes, and, if so, my sympathies are with the working class.' I thought that there was something to be said for this analysis. 'It is a point of view,' said Maurice. I asked him what he did during the strike. 'I stayed here and went on with my work,' he said. It was not quite true. In fact he drove in a car to collect some signatures in favour of a plan of the Archbishop of Canterbury to initiate negotiations for bringing the strike to an end. But his action was not important.

He only began to take a serious interest in politics with the rise of Hitler and National Socialism in Germany. When he stood opposite to them in the trenches he had, as I have said, no animosity against the Germans. The years of his undergraduate career were the years of the collapse of the mark and of the French occupation of the Ruhr. It was then the fashion in liberal university circles, under the influence of Keynes, to think that the French were the villains of the piece and the Germans, now disarmed and harmless, its innocent victims. A Liberal MP, Mr Pringle, came down and told us that we had lost the war, since it had always been British ambition to prevent Europe from being dominated by a single power and as a result of the war it was now dominated by France. It seemed to us the sort of clever paradox that appealed to undergraduates and we were in those days contemptuous of old fuddy-duddies who still thought Germany to be the enemy. It chanced that in 1931 Maurice was enjoying a sabbatical term and he spent a portion of it in the company of a Cambridge friend, Adrian Bishop, in Berlin. They attended a number of Nazi rallies and were greatly horrified and frightened by their brutality and foresaw the all too probable rise to power of the Nazis in Germany and the consequent threat to world peace. He did not, as did left-wing Socialists, see the Nazis as bulwarks of capitalism. To the conflict between Socialism and Capitalism he was indifferent, but what he disliked was physical brutality and the resulting war which it was almost certainly bringing. At that date those in England in academic life had no personal experience of Germany. National Socialism was still comparatively unknown. Opinions upon it varied and in general it was not yet taken very seriously. Maurice Bowra had seen it with his own eyes and took from the first the view that it was a very serious and unmitigated evil. He was dominated by this experience throughout his remaining years.

Some years later at the time of the Spanish Civil War—I suppose in 1938 or so—he said to me, 'I hope that you, as a good Pape, are against a victory for the Fascists in Spain.' I gave a reply that was somewhat equivocal and not wholly satisfactory from his point of view. I argued that, though perhaps there was freer talk on the so-called Loyalist side they talked a good deal of nonsense. 'That does not matter—does not matter in the least,' he said, emphasising the words *in the least*. 'We all talk balls, but what matters is that we should be allowed to talk them.' And indeed that was the truth. His interest was in liberty—in people not being beaten up—and in those who thought that they had a point of view being allowed to express it. He did not profess any great interest in Spain on its intrinsic merits. I do not think that he had ever been to the country and there was in him none of that streak of Hispanidad which one finds in such Englishmen as Walter Starkie or Gerald Brenan or Bevan Wyndham Lewis. He had little doubt that, whoever won the civil war, Spain would still be ruled brutally, incompetently and corruptly. His entire concern was that an ally of Hitler would be established on France's western flank, to her great menace.

About the condition of France at that time he had few illusions. But Léon Blum, an intellectual who moved naturally among intellectuals and held unconventional opinions on such matters as morals, but who allied himself to a working class movement because he thought that with their victory liberty was more likely to survive than under Nazi tyranny, was a man very much to his taste. He was to be supported because in spite of all the incompetence of Blum's government Maurice was gravely shocked by the evidence of well-to-do Frenchmen who preferred their class to their national loyalty and spoke unashamedly of Hitler with admiration as 'one of us, a man who would save the rich from the threats of the working classes'. When the war came he was much disgusted by the tepidity in their support of certain Catholics in England and of the favour which they showed to the Pétainist regime in Vichy. He complained in a number of letters to friends in America that the Catholics were the snakes in the grass in England and inquiring if they were not in all probability the same in America. He was especially incensed by some remarks of which he heard that were made by Robert Sencourt. Years before when Sencourt used to profess the name of Gordon George I asked Maurice what he was by profession. 'He is a charlatan,' he said. 'Anything else?' I asked. 'No,' he said, 'it is a full-time job!'

So long as he was still an undergraduate Maurice Bowra did not very much mix with Dons. His tutor at New College, Joseph, he found stern and forbidding. Later he acquired another tutor, Alic Smith, who was more attractive. The Warden of New College during those days was the extraordinary Spooner, who has enriched the English Dictionary with a word coined after his name, descriptive of his supposed habit of trans-posing the consonants of his words such as saying 'a half-warmed fish' when he meant 'a half-formed wish'. I suppose that on occasion he did make such a transposition but it is not easy to find evidence of anyone who ever actually heard him doing so. An old cousin of mine, a daughter of Dean Church, who lived in the High and enjoyed his friendship for half a century, always maintained that he never perpetrated such sole-cisms. The witticisms which he did perpetrate were far more remarkable —a habit of calculated—or at least apparently calculated—incon-sequence. Thus one day in New College Quad he went up and said to a man, 'Will you come to tea today to meet Mr Hugh Casson?' 'But I am Mr Hugh Casson,' answered the man. 'It doesn't matter,' answered Warden Spooner. 'It doesn't matter a bit. Come to tea just the same.' Maurice Bowra's closest friend among Dons of other Colleges was Robin Dundas, the Censor of Christ Church; he had for him an ironic but deep affection. Dundas was full of curiosity about his pupils and had the habit of cross-questioning those of them who were better looking about the intimate details of their private life. 'The wicked Censor senseth' said Maurice in imitation of 'the wicked grocer' of Chesterton's *Song Against Grocers*. Of his friends at New College, Deane Jones, preceded him into a senior Common Room and became a Fellow of Merton when Maurice was still an undergraduate. I remember a dinner at the Gridiron Club where Deane Jones and Sligger Urquhart, the Dean of Balliol, were seated together at the foot of the table. Maurice was at pains throughout the meal to address them with deep irony as 'our guests, the Dons'.

Such was the distinction of his papers in Mods that he was elected to a Fellowship at Wadham before he had taken his finals in Greats in complete confidence that his papers there would again be of outstanding excellence. He moved to Wadham and remained there for the rest of his life. His social life then divided itself into two parts. There had been those who prophesied that he would not play sufficient part in Wadham's life. Such prophecies proved wholly false. As a Junior Fellow and later as Dean and then Warden he threw himself unstintingly into the College life and entertained the undergraduates without limit. I remember him hurrying home from dinner at the Clarendon on the plea that he must be back in his rooms in order to give port to the College Eight, in whose rowing activities he took no natural interest whatsoever. When he was Warden he entertained at dinner in due rotation all the College freshmen —which was a great deal more than most Heads of Colleges did. At Balliol I never remember under either A. L. Smith or Sandy Lindsay any undergraduate being asked to dine at the Master's Lodgings. The only frequent visitor at A. L. Smith's house was Lewis Namier, then a lecturer but not a Fellow of Balliol, and he was self-invited and by no means welcome. A. L. Smith's daughters composed upon him the verses:

> There once was a scholar called Namier
> Who came 'ere and came 'ere and came 'ere
> And came 'ere and came 'ere and came 'ere
> And came 'ere and came 'ere and came 'ere.

When Maurice was appointed to Wadham he received a letter of congratulation from his tutor, Joseph, on 'going to the most beautiful College in Oxford'. Whatever Magdalen might think there was some justification for the claim. With its original buildings and a garden intact, it was not as extensive as some other Colleges. It was a small College with only just over 100 undergraduates. Although not so very many years before it had had a period of brilliancy when it housed F. E. Smith, John Simon, C. B. Fry and—only slightly less distinguished—F. W. Hirst, it had, by then, fallen from its high estate.

Raymond Asquith said of it, 'Let us not be arrogant. Let us be content to emulate the uncensorious sun that rises over Wadham and sets over Worcester.' Among its small numbers were few who were wealthy or of high lineage or from important public schools. They were of a very different sort from those with whom Bowra had been accustomed to associate up till then. He pursued towards them a definite policy. They were to be given the full measure of his wit and hospitality. On the other hand he was very careful not to admit them to his deep intimacy. 'Never tell them the secrets of your private life,' he said, 'and still more never let them tell their secrets to you.' It was the opposite policy to that adopted by Robin Dundas at Christ Church. The reason for the maxim was, of course, purely one of prudence. An unabashed hedonist, he neither expected nor wished that his pupils should be without their share of adventures, but he saw that it would be merely an embarrassment to them that he should know about them and an obstacle to his authority if they knew about any of his. 'Live and let live' was his motto—to his mind the only sane rule. Among the old alumni it was Birkenhead rather than Simon who mainly attracted him. Birkenhead's habits of life were more to his taste and he was delighted by Margot Asquith's judgment that 'the trouble with Lord Birkenhead is that he is so un-Christ-like'. The judgment seemed to him just, amusing and not unattractive.

As a disciplinarian he was whimsical. He thought that he had a position to maintain and was not prepared to be made ridiculous. My youngest brother, who did not know him nearly as well as I did, was once, when an undergraduate at another College, taken to see him in a somewhat inebriated condition and with his shirt tails hanging out beyond his trousers. 'How dare you come to see me like that?' Maurice thundered and incontinently threw him out. When my nephew remarked to him that I had in later life had a stroke he commented, 'I'm not surprised—not in the least surprised. There was never a glass or a cup that was safe from him if it came within his reach.'

Whenever during his reign as Dean undergraduates applied to him for leave, it was his custom to raise objections, sufficient to show that that such a thing as authority existed, to force them to give such answers as they were capable of but then at the end to give the leave. The undergraduates, at the beginning, understood the game well enough and played it. When towards the end of his term of office he came across a humourless undergraduate of obstinate principle and full of talk about the rights of students, who would not argue, he sighed, thinking that a new and more uncouth generation had arisen. 'I cannot understand them

any longer,' he said. His last term in office as Warden before his compulsory retirement owing to age he spent in a sabbatical escaping
from Oxford. He was in his closing years very deaf and deafness impeded
the easy exchange of conversation which he had previously enjoyed.

It was only natural that during his first years as a Don, Maurice Bowra
while having to play a very full part in the life of Wadham, should also
preserve and form contacts outside the College, which were to enable
him over the years to become the leading figure in Oxford life. His
friend Deane Jones once said, 'No one ever really goes down,' and it is
true that, as perhaps at all times, men of scholarly interests tended on one
excuse or another to hang about the city, never fully able to tear themselves away. Yet after a time his friends of the Essay Society had dis-
persed and Maurice had called in a number of new friends slightly his
junior and who had not overlapped with him as an undergraduate, to
take their places. There was Cyril Connolly at Balliol with whom his
relations, as Winston Churchill said of Baldwin, had their ups and
downs, the downs perhaps on the whole predominating. There was a
time during which in revenge for Maurice's sharp tongue Connolly used
to call him 'Mr Bowra the boarer,' a title invented, it is said, by Colonel
Kolkhorst the Chaucerian don. I have heard that it was Maurice Bowra
who said of Connolly that he was the cleverest undergraduate of his
time, but I fancy, that it was, in fact, Kenneth Clark who said that. Any-
way all, whether of eulogy or of denigration was in the end forgotten.
Then there was Kenneth Clark himself, the aesthete son of rich philistine
parents, whose survey of the pictures of civilisation has, of course, today
won him such unusual acclaim from the devotees of television. There
was John Sparrow, now the Warden of All Souls, where he succeeded
the very distinguished Humphrey Sumner. 'One Sparrow does not make
a Sumner,' said Maurice on the news of his election. There was Henry
Yorke who won distinction as a novelist under the name of Henry Green.
There was John Betjeman—'a man', said Maurice, 'of extraordinary
originality,' but whose genius did not win favour with the University
authorities. He quarrelled with his tutor C. S. Lewis who absurdly
thought him a 'pretentious playboy'. A religious devotee, then, as he is
now, he unfortunately failed in the absurd examination of Divvers on the
books of the New Testament, which was then of obligation for all undergraduates. Later in his career Evelyn Waugh came into Maurice's life.
Their paths had not much, if at all, crossed when they were undergraduates. They preserved relations of friendship on the whole but again, as
with Cyril Connolly, Maurice's relations with Evelyn were equivocal,

marked with ups and downs, as neither of them much troubled to hold
back the barbed comments that came so readily to their lips. Maurice was
beyond question Samgrass, the worldly Don so mercilessly satirised in
*Brideshead Revisited*. 'A Waugh to end Waugh,' said Maurice of Evelyn's
*Sword of Honour*, when Francis King was so injudicious as to praise that
trilogy. In his notorious diaries we find Evelyn professing to have
exposed Maurice's pretended knowledge of the poetry of all languages
as portentous fraud. 'Bowra is greatly lacking in frankness,' he wrote,
'and it came to me that all his appreciation for foreign poetry was an
imposture. I questioned him sharply on his knowledge of Lorca and
found his answers unsatisfactory!' Then there was Hugh Gaitskell,
except for Bob Boothby, his only political friend, and for whose devo-
tion to the Labour cause he had high respect. Among aesthetes there
was Harold Acton, in many ways the best-known undergraduate of his
generation and Brian Howard, like Byron, 'mad, bad and dangerous to
know'. There was Isaiah Berlin, strange immigrant from Riga who
survived to become President of Wolfson College and to pronounce the
panegyric at Maurice's funeral. There was David Cecil who was attracted
by him to the academic life and who joined him as a colleague at Wadham. There was Edgar Lobel, a strange scholarly figure of uncertain
racial origin who, so the learned told us, was, in contrast to Maurice with
his love of the literary and political significance of the classics, the model
of exact scholarship, editing broken papyri with their Greek fragments.
'The purest scholar of our time,' confessed Maurice. He was not a
member of the regular University establishment, holding only an ill-paid
job as an assistant at the Bodleian. He was afterwards made a University
reader. Within his classical ambit he was full of contempt for any who
fell short of the highest standards of accuracy, but he compensated for
this by cursory and very irresponsible talk on matters with which he had
no concern. I remember his objection to Cyril Bailey's sentimental
rhetoric in praise of high mountains. 'A mountain top always seems to
me just like a field,' he said. I cannot imagine what he meant. I also heard
him asked at a jovial dinner-party what would be the effect of the splitting
of the atom. 'Oh, two atoms would grow, where at present we only have
one,' he answered airily. 'Otherwise no difference at all.' It is only fair
to say that, from what I have read, Lord Rutherford held very much the
same opinion.

The three older Dons who had the greatest influence on Maurice
Bowra were Professor Lindemann, Gilbert Murray and Sandy Lindsay.
To all of them his reaction was equivocal. Lindemann was, like Lobel, of

foreign origin and education. His family came from Baden-Baden but
were resident in Alsace and opted for French nationality in 1870. He had
a very distinguished record as a research pilot for the Royal Flying
Corps during the First War and afterwards came to Oxford as Professor
of Experimental Philosophy. His position at Oxford was anomalous
since he held Fellowship both at Christ Church and at Wadham. He
lived at Christ Church but came across from time to time to dine (off an
extraordinary vegetarian menu) at Wadham. He enjoyed public notice
and rather childish exhibitionism. I first met him at the table of Edward
Marjoribanks, Lord Hailsham's half-brother. It was his great delight to
frighten with alarming prophecies ill-educated young ladies of high
social pretensions. 'And what will happen then, Professor?' they asked.
'Oh, then the whole universe will disintegrate,' he would reply with a
beaming smile. He was certainly never married and, as far as one knows,
had no active sexual life, but it gave him great pleasure to raise his eye-
brows in pretended shock as he attached a hidden Freudian meaning to
every innocent action of his colleagues, such as the opening of a door.
'We all know what that means,' he said. He interested himself greatly in
the filling of the vacancy at Wadham, taking strongly the line that an
experienced scientist should be appointed and thus opposing Bowra's
application. He took no interest in literature, classical or modern. He was
a man of no religion and a very strict materialist, arguing that, if only he
were allowed to do certain experiments, he could turn any ordinary
person into a musician of the quality of Beethoven.

'Of all sexual actions copulation is the least deleterious,' I once heard
George Moore say. Lindemann would not agree. For some reason,
though he repudiated with scorn all religious beliefs, yet he took an
unyieldingly rigid line about any straightforward sexual activities and
Maurice and he soon found themselves in conflict over the treatment
which the College should mete out to an undergraduate who had put a
girl in the family way. Their relations at the time were not cordial. Later
on they improved when over the Nazi issue Bowra of course became a
very strong enemy of appeasement while Lindemann was the close
friend, collaborator and scientific adviser of Churchill. When in 1938
the Wardenship of Wadham fell vacant, Lindemann busied himself in
supporting Bowra's election and had a great part in bringing it about.
With the war, as is known, Lindemann was conscribed into Churchill's
government and played a very prominent part in organising the city-
bombing of Germany in the closing years of the war. Bowra made no
pretence of an understanding of scientific processes—he was never able

even to drive a motor car—and I do not think that he claimed himself competent to hold an opinion on any of the questions which caused bitter division between Lindemann and Sir Henry Tizard. But, when Lindemann was away in London, Bowra's feelings towards him cooled somewhat. He was disappointed that he himself was not asked to perform any service for the Government in the war and perhaps thought that Lindemann should have done more for him than he did. When Lindemann was raised to the peerage as Lord Cherwell, Mr Anthony Powell, who chanced to be lunching with Maurice records that Maurice said, 'Don't mind that—don't mind it at all. You wouldn't believe the fuss it has caused.' There was, he confessed 'bad blood' about it and he delighted in playing the old game with cherry stones to the count of 'Tinker, tailor, soldier, sailor, rich man, poor man, Lindemann, thief.'

Maurice of course wrote prolifically on matters of classical literature. On the merits of these works I am quite incompetent to pass a judgment nor would it lie within the scope of this book to attempt to do so. But it was commonly said both by his friends and others that his prose was strangely undistinguished in contrast with the brilliance of his conversation and even with his frequently somewhat indecent private poems. For instance his parody of Newman, of which the first line runs 'Lead, blindly tight, amid the revolving room,' is one of the few that can be printed! His friend, John Sparrow, said of him that 'his prose was unreadable and his verse was unprintable'.

At the time that he was an undergraduate Gilbert Murray was the Regius Professor of Greek. It is not customary for Regius Professors to take private pupils but in the disorganisation as Oxford started up again after the war Gilbert Murray consented to take a few clever pupils. Maurice Bowra was of their number. Murray's poetical approach to Greek literature as opposed to the dry dustiness of the rigid pedants greatly appealed to Maurice and he became a fervent admirer and a favourite pupil. When Murray stood as Liberal candidate for the University seat and was defeated Maurice remarked that he should have stood for an intellectual constituency. He was a frequent visitor to the Murray home on Boars Hill. It was a great tribute of discipleship that he was so, since the household was one of vegetarian and teetotal habits that were by no means those to which Maurice was accustomed. In 1936 Murray had reached the age limit and had to give up his Professorship. The appointment was a royal appointment and Baldwin, who was the Prime Minister, delegated to Murray the task of finding a successor for himself. Maurice Bowra was confident that he would be appointed, but to his surprise

Murray nominated E. R. Dodds, the Professor of Greek at Birmingham. Maurice took it hardly, the more so since it was by no means made clear to him why he had been passed over. 'Of course,' he said, 'the reason is that I write too much, but why couldn't he say that? Why couldn't he say, "He writes too much"?' Others in Oxford—for instance Cyril Bailey at Balliol—told him that it might prove to be a blessing in disguise, and this indeed it certainly proved to be, for, had he become the Regius Professor, he could not have been elected Warden of Wadham when that position fell vacant a few years later, and it is certainly in that position that he was happiest and made his distinguished contribution to Oxford life as the University's Vice-Chancellor. Great scholar that he was, he was greater as an administrator.

Sandy Lindsay was the Master of Balliol. With him as with Lindemann, though for very different reasons, his relations were equivocal. He did not like him as a man. Their temperaments were very different. Lindsay was a Lowland Scot, a Presbyterian minister, who combined his Presbyterianism with the ethical theories of Immanuel Kant in a not very effective amalgam. His attitude towards the Bible was well illustrated when there was some act of immorality among the Balliol undergraduates. It was by no means certain that the undergraduate who was accused was the real culprit. Yet Sandy Lindsay insisted that he be punished and sent down. He quoted to the other Fellows the text 'It is expedient that one man should die for the people.' His conscience apparently demanded that it should fortify itself by a biblical text. Whether the words quoted were in the Bible spoken by Christ or against Christ was a matter of total indifference. When later he was raised to the peerage Maurice treated his elevation as a matter of great ridicule and used to refer to him as Lord Ecclefechan. Yet though he did not like him as a man or think highly of him as a philosopher he recognised his effectiveness as a University administrator. 'Look here, Bowra,' Maurice used to parody him as he unrolled his schemes for turning the University into a Workers' Training College. 'The Master of Balliol', he pronounced, 'has been ill but is unfortunately getting better.' But Maurice confessed that, though their tussles were many, Sandy Lindsay usually won.

Lindsay was of course a Liberal-Labour in politics and shortly after Munich, Bourne, the Conservative Member for Oxford, died. The critics of Munich decided to make the by-election a test case of the popularity of Chamberlain's policies. Quintin Hogg was the official Conservative candidate. Lindsay stood against him as a critic of Munich, and a number of figures in the academic world, among whom Maurice was prominent, gave their support to Lindsay. But the backlash against Munich was not by then fully developed. Hogg won fairly easily. It was Maurice's only essay into practical politics, of which he always pretended that he had no understanding.

In the early 1920's religious belief was very rare among undergraduates—rarer than it is today, when it is commoner among the pupils than among their Dons—and Maurice Bowra was of course only typical of his generation in having no religious faith. He differed from his fellows in that, while they were most of them agnostics in reaction from their public school religion and from the belief of their parents, he had been brought up from first youth by a father who called himself a Huxleyan agnostic. How far it was a close study of Thomas Huxley which had led him to such a conclusion or how far he reached agnosticism through a general belief in the impossibility of knowledge, I cannot say. Certainly Maurice Bowra had little scientific interest and I do not fancy that it was any detailed study of biological discoveries which led him to a lack of faith. But he was not for that powerful in his hostility to religion. Though in general of liberal opinions, he had early discovered, as many had discovered before him, that often those who professed principles of universal benevolence, compensated themselves for their principles and are in fact less generous to their neighbours and those in need than their more conservative and less ideological fellow citizens. So equally he had noticed that, though there were such things as religious fanaticism and clerical bigotry, yet the enemies of religion were sometimes more bitter in their hostility than its friends in their championship. We thought for a time of producing in a somewhat satirical fashion a pro-God number of the *Oxford Outlook* to rebuke and mock at the anti-godders. But the project was not very serious and never came to anything.

Among his friends of the New College Essay Society only Eric Strauss and Douglas Woodruff were Catholics. Douglas Woodruff was never a very intimate friend, Strauss he welcomed for his mastery of 'magnificent nonsense' and a little complained—though not very deeply—of his habit of attempting to convert his friends when he fell into serious conversation. There were other younger friends—Cuthbert Fitzherbert-Brockholes and Michael Trappes-Lomax whom he was always careful to introduce with some irony as members of 'old Catholic families'. Piers Synott was also a friend. Jack Haldane was the most fanatical enemy of religion among his friends, and Maurice said to him one day, 'Of course all that you say is true, but, mark my words, you and I will both die screaming for a priest.' Of course it in no way happened like this to either of them, and I do not suppose that Maurice ever imagined that it would, or intended that it should. He simply said it to annoy!

He had inherited agnosticism from his father and, confronted with the claims of Christianity, he did not find them sufficient or convincing. He did not find them true, and he had no wish to find them true. To Blougram's 'Has it your vote to be so if it can?' he gave a resounding 'No.' For he was a lover of the hedonistic life and unsympathetic to those claims for asceticism which might challenge his freedom to enjoy himself. Of the rival Christian claimants the Protestants were more to be condemned for their hostility to drink, the Catholics for their hostility to sex. When he was established at Wadham he developed a great institutional loyalty to the College. Though he had defied the regulation about attending chapel when he was at New College, he was a regular attendant at Wadham, though he had no wish to impose compulsion on the undergraduates. He attended chapel not so much as an act of worship as an expression of College loyalty. He supported his successor as Vice-Chancellor in his wish to continue the custom of opening the meetings of Heads of Colleges with prayer and was careful at all times to recite the Lord's Prayer in a robustly loud voice in his support. I do not suppose that he ever communicated nor is there any reason to think that he ever wavered in his fundamental agnosticism. When he was elected Warden of Wadham some friends at Merton gave him a celebratory dinner. After dinner they debouched into the College Chapel and indulged in some irreverent horseplay—according to one story they celebrated what they pretended to be a Black Mass, but I doubt that. It ended by Maurice ascending the pulpit and delivering a mock sermon, which was only interrupted by the intervention of a rebuking verger. It was said to be the only occasion in history when a Head of a College was rebuked for brawling in church. But that is not so; I was myself present when Maurice attended the Confirmation of Penelope Betjeman in Blackfriars. He seated himself at the back and before the ceremony commenced indulged in high-spirited and good-humoured raillery. A lay brother who doubtless 'wist not that it was' the Vice-Chancellor, came up and told him to make less noise.

Maurice developed at Wadham a friendship with Brabant, the College chaplain, with whom he had large arguments on Brabant's High Church theories of Church authority, which of course Maurice was not prepared to concede. He was of the opinion that the survival of society depended on the survival of high scholarship and therefore had a prejudice against parsons or priests of high scholarly attainments who sacrificed those attainments to what he thought of as the lesser task of evangelisation, who had, as he put it with some bitterness, 'no respect for scholarship'. He regretted Penelope Betjeman's submission to Rome but it did not in any way interfere with his friendship.

It was not, I think, until the rise of the totalitarian regimes that he admitted any especial prejudice against the Catholic Church, which he thought to be very insufficiently active against the plainly anti-Christian policies of Hitler and to a lesser extent of Mussolini and Franco. When the war ended his interest in such policies abated and his last action was to sign a letter, along with many others, which only appeared after his death, against what he wrongly imagined to be the abolition of the Latin Mass by the Second Vatican Council. As I do not suppose that he very often heard Mass either in English or in Latin, it may be wondered why he interested himself in the controversy. But by that closing stage of his life, though still the unyielding friend of liberty, he had come to think that the structure of society was weakened by unending innovation. He did not wish those who were not Catholics to join the Church or to conform to its teaching. But let those within the Church continue to do as they had always done and not confound all by ceaseless changes.

He hated but accepted death as regrettable but inevitable. The last time that I met him was at a dinner-party. He was most genial and friendly and as we parted I expressed the hope that we would soon meet again. 'I don't suppose so,' he said. 'We will both soon be dead.' He always hoped that he would have a sudden and painless death and this was granted to him.

# Leslie Hore-Belisha

Talk of court news; and we'll talk with them too—
Who loses and who wins; who's in, who's out—
And take upon's the mystery of things.
　　　　　　　　　　　　*King Lear*—Shakespeare

The Union, like so much else at Oxford, had come to an end during the
First World War. A few of its rooms were reserved for Life Members,
who wished to use its library, but the buildings in general were turned
into an Officers' Mess. No debates took place. With the armistice and the
return of the undergraduates it was natural that its life should be revived.
But it was also uncertain what its future would be in this new world of
the post-war period. Party politics, upon which its life was so largely
based, had been suspended throughout the nation during the war. The
1918 election indeed showed clearly enough that we were to have party
politics again, but in what form we were to have them was far from
certain. Undergraduates before the war had been brought up on the
Gilbertian formula that they were all born to be either little Liberals or
else little Conservatives. Even after the war Oxford undergraduates still
as a general rule adhered to the traditional formula, but it was now Labour
rather than the Liberals who were the official opposition. It is true that
Labour undergraduates at the Union were still comparatively a rarity and
we had to wait for some years until the Union had in Kenneth Lindsay
its first Labour President. But apart from its party allegiance the general
future of the Union in Oxford life was also in the balance.

The Union had always occupied a somewhat equivocal position in
Oxford—to some the object of intense ambition, to others a place for
contempt and ridicule, where career-chasing little boys who had not yet
grown up or learnt to know the world played with the notion that they
were already important statesmen. It was generally thought that the

highest years of the Union's life had been the closing years of the nineteenth century when F. E. Smith, John Simon and Hilaire Belloc had
been there and had been in turns its President, but even of those years
F. E. Smith, by then Lord Birkenhead, had said at the Union Centenary
Banquet in 1923, 'Whenever you deal with any particular period in the
history of the Union, you always find that the intellectuals of the period
disparage it as a contemptible institution. When I was at Oxford and used
to speak at the Union, as I speak today, we were always told that it was
an inferior place. There have always been a few intellectuals who have
refused to take part in the debates. Lord Morley never spoke until he had
become a figure in the larger sphere of public life. Lord Randolph
Churchill never opened his mouth in this hall until he again was a leader
of a great section of the Unionist party. I cannot help thinking that both
would have been the gainers had they been debaters in this hall. Lord
Morley would have gained in flippancy. Lord Randolph Churchill
would have gained in earnestness.' In fact Lord Morley did once speak at
the Union but without any success and Lord Randolph was expelled
from the Society for failing to pay his subscription. It has been much the
same with the Union's reputation in these inter-war and post-war years.
Oxford during those years produced six Prime Ministers—Macmillan,
Attlee, Douglas-Home, Eden, Heath and Wilson. Of those six Macmillan had frequented the Union, though mainly as a Liberal and sometimes as a Socialist, before the war and had risen to be Secretary.
Doubtless he would have become President in due course had his
career not been interrupted, but he did not return to Oxford after the
war to complete his course. Of the Labour Prime Ministers neither
Attlee nor Wilson ever went to the Union, nor among other Labour
politicians did Gaitskell or Crossman. Eden never joined the Union and
only visited it once when he gate-crashed a debate upon the League of
Nations that was addressed by Lord Robert Cecil. Douglas-Home
never, I think, joined. Edward Heath alone among Prime Ministers of
recent years was, in his time, President of the Union.

Hore Belisha became its first post-war President in 1919. He was
succeeded by the very unpolitical Thomas Earp, whose distinction was
won in art criticism and the Union had to wait until 1924 for another
President—Gerald Gardiner—who was destined to be a Cabinet
Minister, as Lord Chancellor and not as a run of the mill politician—nor
indeed a run of the mill President, for he was, I think, the only President
of the Union who was ever sent down during his term of office. After
him Lennox-Boyd, Hailsham, Boyd-Carpenter, Michael Stewart and

Greenwood have in addition to Heath risen from the Presidential chair to a Cabinet seat. There are a number of others who have reached the Cabinet and who in their day were prominent at the Union, though they never reached the Presidency. The Union personnel changed from the pre-war days. When I myself stood for the first time for the Presidency, I felt, to be frank, quite confident of victory and was surprised and humiliated to be defeated by Gordon Bagnall, who was the son of a Nonconformist Minister. I was the more surprised to be told that a number of members had voted against me on the ground that I was an Etonian and that they were not going to have the Union run by toffs. It was felt that in the past it had been a preserve of the upper classes and now the newly emerging proletariat were going to make good their challenge to this citadel of privilege. It had never occurred to me that I was a gentleman nor had my company ever consisted predominantly of Etonians. But, when I came to think of it, those with whom I associated were almost entirely of some sort of public school or another. I had more sympathy with the members' revolt against the public schools than they can have guessed.

I frequently hear people who say that the Union is in a bad way and by no means what it was. As the quotation from Lord Birkenhead shows, people have always been saying that since the Society began. Whether it is at all true I am in no position to say. I have over the years had the privilege of knowing a number of its Presidents and have been invited to take part in, I suppose, some five or six of its debates. I can only say that I have without exception received every courtesy and hospitality from a wide variety of former Presidents and have always found its debates, whatever I may have heard about rumours of what happened upon other occasions, conducted with proper decency and consideration. The arrangements in general have changed remarkably little. The whole catalogue of undergraduate officers—President, Treasurer, Librarian, Secretary, Standing Committee, Library Committee—were in 1919 restored exactly as they had been ever since 1841 and as indeed they remain today, although no longer 'junior'.

> At the Union, I'm assured,
> There's a Bursar and a Steward,
> A Committee, which occasionally commeets,
> A President besides,
> Who presumably presides,
> While the Secretary invariably secretes.

As soon as the war ended it was decided with obvious propriety to restart the Society's debates. The first problem was how to provide the Society with the appropriate authorities, Dr Nathaniel Micklem, of Mansfield, had been the President in 1911 and he volunteered to act as a temporary President in order to inculcate in the Members the rules of debate and the customs of the Society. He did so by general agreement with supreme tact and ability. But, when his term was finished, it was obviously the time to elect a proper President. The two most prominent debaters of the Society's opening term were Hore-Belisha and Reggie Harris, the nephew of Schiller, the pragmatist Don of Corpus Christi, himself to be soon afterwards a Fellow of All Souls. Harris was representative of the Conservatives, and Belisha the Liberals. They were personally friendly enough and used to dine together before the debates. But when the election came Belisha was victorious and thus became the Society's first post-war President. He very completely stamped his flamboyant personality upon post-war Oxford.

The Union, like other institutions, is of course more outspoken in its topics and manner of debate today in our permissive society than it was in the era of Hore-Belisha. The rules against theological motions have been repealed. Such matters as birth control, abortion, or euthanasia are freely debated. Whether conduct is today more unrestrained than it used to be, whether bawdy jokes are more appreciated when they no longer have the cachet of being at all risqué, it is not for this essay to inquire. Habits are today slightly less formal. Today only the officers wear white ties. Visiting speakers are accepted in a dinner jacket. Yet substantially all is unchanged. Today the President has his private office equipped with a private telephone, upon which he appears to talk quite unceasingly. During my own Presidency I cannot remember once speaking on the telephone.

Belisha did not very flagrantly challenge the conventions in his own day. I remember Christopher Scaife, who was to succeed me in the Presidency and who was at Belisha's own College of St. John's, once professing to be shocked at some of the *bons mots* of one of Belisha's speeches, but I confess that I could not see anything in them at which it was possible to take exception. Belisha had used in his speech the phrase Homo Sapiens. A facetious member on the bench opposite shouted 'Translate.' 'Homo Sapiens,' said Belisha, 'clever bugger.' But surely one had to be very strait-laced to take exception to such a repartee.

The Union's greatest hour of notoriety, if not of fame, was to come

some ten years later in 1933 when it passed the famous motion, expressing its unwillingness to fight for King and Country. At that period, the
Union, largely under the influence of Mr Michael Stewart, had imposed
upon its deliberation a manner more earnest and serious than that to
which those accustomed to Oxford's tradition so largely re-created by
Belisha, had been used. This motion about King and country was copied
in very many countries all over the world and was interpreted as an
unwillingness to resist Nazi pressure and as such was alleged—probably wrongly—to have played a part in encouraging Hitler in his aggres-
sion. Whatever the use that was made of the motion, the debate itself,
which took place very soon after Hitler's accession to power had no
reference at all to the desirability of fighting against Hitler but was
entirely concerned with the necessity of fighting against Communist
Russia. Pacifist motions had often before been debated by the Unions.
The Cambridge Union had for instance passed a motion of quite un-
qualified non-resistance in 1927, nor did the Oxford motion at first
arouse any great interest nor would it have aroused any great interest had
it not been for the subsequent folly of Randolph Churchill and some
very right-wing and allegedly Mosleyite toughs in attempting to disrupt
the Society's business by defacing its minutes.

One of the most controversial figures in Oxford in Belisha's time was
Dr Farnell, the Rector of Exeter and Vice-Chancellor. He attempted to
impose upon the undergraduates a somewhat wooden discipline, which
might have been suitable for boys coming up directly from school but
which was hardly acceptable to warriors returning from the trenches.
Before the war he had crossed swords with Lord Hugh Cecil, bitterly
opposing Cecil's candidacy as a Burgess for the University. After the
war, when he was Vice-Chancellor, Cecil had his tit-for-tat. Farnell
sought to ban a project for an Oxford and Cambridge aeroplane race.
Cecil arranged for the race to take place during the vacation near
London and under the patronage of the Duke of York. Farnell also gave
offence by neglecting to include invitations to the University Burgesses
to take part in the procession when the University presented a formal
address to the King. He suppressed a paper, put a ban on lectures by
Bertrand Russell and attempted to suppress a birth control meeting to be
addressed by Marie Stopes. Feelings ran high. A box of chocolates was
presented to him which, it was reported—I think without foundation—
had been doctored by powdered glass. Belisha took part in the general
campaign for greater freedom but in a good-humoured fashion and,
though he wrote and spoke against Farnell, prided himself on preserving

friendly personal relations and boasted how on a visit to Oxford the only house at which he had been entertained to a meal was the Vice-Chancellor's. He had no intention of making Oxford the battlefield of his serious conflicts.

Belisha was of a Jewish Sephardic family. His father, whose ambitions were military, had died of a stroke when he was a little boy, and he had been brought up by his mother, to whom he was throughout her life most deeply devoted. He was sent to school to Clifton at the Jewish house, where he showed himself mainly notable neither for games, which he on the whole despised, nor for academic work, which he took lightly, but for his remarkable oratorical powers. He was frankly ambitious and made no bones about it that he saw himself as a future Disraeli, destined to play a similar part in the national life to that of his great Jewish prototype. He had arranged to go up to Oxford to St John's College, but before he arrived there the war broke out. He at once joined up, served in France, being engaged in the heavy fighting at Neuve-Chapelle. He was then sent to Greece and Salonika to serve on the staff of General Milne. He rose to the rank of Major, 'the smiling Major', as he liked to call himself on his later election addresses, and was invalided out as a sufferer from malaria in March, 1918. He became a King's Messenger. With the armistice he went up to Oxford to St. John's.

At first he was disillusioned. He wrote of his returning generation in the *Oxford Outlook* of May 1919, 'We came back. But it was by the waters of Isis that we sat down and wept when we remembered Oxford. In truth we were all ill at ease in the Zion of our longing. A new generation had sprung up in the land—a generation puny in numbers and perhaps for that very reason more sedulous of Dons and ritual, more Pharasaic than the Pharisee—and we came as ghosts to trouble joy. And some hardly recognised Oxford. But we too were unrecognisable.' To be frank, it is not very clear what this is supposed to mean and to whom it is referring. But it certainly meant that he was not prepared to take his standards from anybody else, but was determined to carve out a career for himself. He chose the Union as the theatre on which he was best suited to succeed. Louis Golding heard one of his speeches. Golding had got as far as the Union's paper before the war but never took part in its debates when he returned after the war. But he records of Belisha: 'He was respected and envied. He was witty, devastatingly witty, with an irony no one wished to provoke. He could hold his audience spellbound. I remember one evening at the Union we were all listening spellbound to Hore-Belisha. He had worked up to a tremendous peroration, but with his arm uplifted to deliver it, he seemed to remember something, for he walked down from the platform and out of the room. The House sat in absolute silence during the minute or two that he was away. Then he returned and finished his speech to applause that one rarely heard.' This is, I think, just enough, both paying tribute to his brilliance of expression and the flamboyant and perhaps sometimes rather absurd gimmicks which he was prepared when necessary to employ. Oxford on the whole enjoyed both and he played up to Oxford.

He had not very much money to spare, but he was reckless in his expenditure. His rooms were furnished with innumerable purple cushions and lighted with lamps mounted upon brackets of curved Venetian bronze. He entertained with magnificence, dealing out magnums of champagne and Turkish coffee made in pots that he had brought back from Salonika. He joined the Archery Club, which gave splendid lunches in St John's and afterwards adjourned to draw an unsteady bow at the target which had been erected on the College lawn. His walls were lined with beautifully and expensively bound books—books of which it was commonly believed that they were more frequently displayed than their contents studied. He was not then thought of as a wide reader, and, as with many other prominent undergraduates of the day, academic demands did not sit very heavily on him. He tried to pose as a reformer, but most of us, I fancy, thought of him as an exuberant adventurer, not perhaps unprincipled, but a man upon whom opinions did not sit so very heavily. It was his ambition not merely to become President of the Union but also to impose himself upon the Union as the leading personality of his generation. In this he was, on the whole and within his particular circle, successful. For some years after he had gone down he was both a most constant visitor as a guest at Union debates and at various Oxford clubs and dinners. Four terms after him Beverley Nichols was elected to the Union's Presidency and he took the very controversial step of inviting Horatio Bottomley down to debate before the Society as its guest. Visitors were in those days a rarity—only one, or at the most two a term—and invitations, it was generally thought, should be reserved for people of great respectability and distinction. Visitors did not come down, as they do today, week after week and for every debate, when undergraduates no longer care to tolerate a debate unassisted by guests. Horatio Bottomley was, it is true, at that time a Member of Parliament and had not yet met with his final and irrevocable disgrace. But he had been bankrupted and was generally thought of as a far from respectable character. 'I have never', he laughingly told the

House, 'enjoyed greater affluence than when I was living as an undis-charged bankrupt.' Life Members thought that it was in the worst of taste to parade such a boast before the Oxford Union.

Beverley Nichols was widely criticised for the invitation. But, if Bottomley was to come, it was agreed that Hore-Belisha was the obvious speaker to oppose him. Hore-Belisha had adopted and employed as well as, if not better than any other young man of that day, the Union habits of epigram and flippancy which derived so very largely from the tradition of Philip Guedalla. As was the general custom of the day, he professed himself an Asquithian Liberal and made no concealment of his ultimate political ambitions. But he was always ready enough to talk on any non-political topic and to garnish his discourse with the traditional Union phraseology. I remember a debate 'That this House would rather have a First than a Blue.' Hore Belisha, though he had no great ambition for either of such achievements, championed the Firsts. He decried Blues, expatiating on the glories of a First and explaining that in contrast 'men had bolted from a Blue'. Bottomley sat in Parliament as an Independent Member and professed to advocate a not very well-defined scheme for a Business Government. Belisha for that evening at any rate, appeared as a party man. He had beforehand taken the advice of friends whether it would be wise to employ against Bottomley the well-known lines from Hamlet about Horatio. They had advised against them as too trite and he had taken their advice, but on his feet he got carried away, and after having criticised Bottomley, pronounced 'There are more things in heaven and earth, Horatio.' There was an immense outburst of laughter and Belisha astutely sat down, not even concluding the quotation. On the train back to London Bottomley attempted to sell him some shares.

Belisha was—so we thought in those days, somewhat of a seeker after causes to afford him a platform rather than a firm believer in them. He took up with the Anti-Waste campaign in whose name Lord Rother-mere was at the time running candidates, demanding reduction in government expenditure. When that met with no great success he became an extreme supporter of *laissez-faire* and opponent of any sort of government interference in industry. He came down to Oxford and addressed the newly formed Russell and Palmerston Club on this topic.

The Asquithian Liberals were at that time most anxious to rebuild their very fallen fortunes. They were prodigal in their offers of candi-dacies to young undergraduates down from Oxford or Cambridge, but it was naturally a great deal easier to become a Liberal candidate than to

be elected a Liberal Member. Lord Gladstone, who was then Chairman of
the Liberal Party, asked Belisha if he would become the Liberal candidate
at Devonport at the election which was then threatening owing to the
imminent fall of Lloyd George's Coalition. In the 1918 election the
Liberal candidate in that constituency had lost his deposit and Belisha
had no personal connection with Devonport. Nevertheless he eagerly
accepted and sent telegrams to his friends at St John's bidding them
come down to help him. As his great friend Herbert Finberg wryly told
me, in his telegram he announced that he was a candidate but omitted as
totally unimportant to say what party he was championing. He found an
old stage coach in a backyard, harnessed four horses to it and drove it
through the town. To questions his invariable answer was 'Let the will
of the people prevail.' He was asked whether he supported local option
about the opening of pubs—an issue which was at that time prominent
in Liberal programmes but one with which Belisha had by nature little
sympathy. 'What's the good of asking me what I think about local
option?' he answered. 'I mean one thing by it and you mean another.
What I say is, let the will of the people prevail.' He was not victorious
in that election but he succeeded in bringing down the Conservative
majority from 9,125 to 1,921 and, when in 1923 there was another election on Baldwin's proposal to introduce protective tariffs, Belisha easily
won the seat as a Liberal free trader and held it for twenty-two years until
his eventual defeat in the Labour landslide of 1945.

It would be quite beyond the ambit of this book to follow through in
any detail the ups and downs of his turbulent and colourful political
career. The Liberals of course only emerged as the third party from the
election of 1923. Belisha's first important decision after his election was
then to decide whether to give his support to a Labour or a Conservative
Government. As a supporter of *laissez-faire* he was opposed alike to
protection and to socialism. In the dilemma he followed Asquith's
invitation and gave his vote for the establishment of a minority Labour
Government. From 1923 to 1931 he did not play any very prominent
part in national politics. He was mainly concerned to make himself a
popular constituency Member and ostentatiously supported the naval
building programme, announcing that he would never give a vote
against the adequate defences of the country but being accused by some
more pacifist Liberals of being more concerned in winning constituency
favour than in espousing Liberal policies. In the confusions of 1930 and
1931 for a time he toyed with the New Party and Sir Oswald Mosley.
Harold Nicolson in his *Diaries* records as late as July 22, 1931, that Hore-

Belisha 'has joined us in spirit and hopes to bring with him a group of Liberals. He will remain in the Liberal camp for the present and work with us there.' But when a few months later MacDonald's Government fell, he came out as the most vigorous of the National Liberal supporters of Sir John Simon in the National Government and, when that Government was formed he received office in it and remained in office up till his dismissal by Neville Chamberlain during the Second World War. He was valuable to the Government in subordinate posts, especially as Financial Secretary to the Treasury because of his ready fertility in debate, and, when he became Minister of Transport his flamboyant flair for self-advertisement was useful both to the Government and to himself. He was determined to reduce the heavy toll of road casualties and decorated our streets with what were known as Belisha Beacons in order to protect the pedestrians who wanted to cross the road.

Under Chamberlain he became Secretary for War, entrusted with the task of bringing the army up to readiness for war. His policy at the War Office aroused much controversy. He received much praise and later much criticism. Eventually Chamberlain demanded his resignation, owing, as was generally thought, to the hostility of the regular officers and the commanders in the field. As one of the more distinguished of them explained, 'We do not pretend to judge the niceties of these intricate controversies, but what we want to know is, is the bugger a shit?' Into the controversies of his administration it would be quite beyond the purposes of this book to enter. When Churchill succeeded Chamberlain as Prime Minister he did not give Belisha office and Belisha was indeed a frequent and trenchant critic of the Churchill administration, but on the formation of the Caretaker Government Belisha became Minister of National Insurance. The reign of that Government was of course only a matter of months and in the election of 1945 Belisha lost his seat at Devonport. He afterwards fought a gay but unsuccessful battle at Coventry. Some of the ballot papers went astray and Belisha, jaunty in adversity, quipped, 'There's a shortage of everything under Socialism. There's even a shortage of ballot papers.' He was created a peer in 1954 and in 1957 died of a sudden heart attack while making a speech in favour of British–French friendship at Rheims.

It was generally thought that Hore Belisha was a confirmed bachelor. The full story of Violet Trefusis' Lesbian relations with Vita Sackville-West, the wife of Harold Nicolson, subsequently revealed by Nigel Nicolson, was not then generally public. Yet it was not thought probable that Belisha's friendship with Violet Trefusis would lead to any serious consequences. He gave unstintingly of his affection to his widowed mother Lady Hore, but it was the common opinion that ambition was his ruling passion and that he was not willing to abandon prospects of success for the joys of matrimony. However in 1936 his mother died, and although the years of his most colourful and controversial politics were still before him, he then, by his own claim made at the time of his dismissal from the War Office, abandoned conventional ambition. Yet, throughout all the War Office years he still remained a bachelor and it was only in 1944, when out of office and a little apparently in the doldrums that he, to most people's surprise, contracted his very happy marriage to Cynthia Elliot. In the same way to his casual friends, if not, it may be, to his intimate acquaintances he always appeared in early and Oxford days a creature irretrievably terrestrial. He spoke freely of ambition and in moments off-parade spoke of it with flippancy. He had for religion the respect that one might easily have found in a well-bred and cultured agnostic. For instance, he satirised the modernist profession of faith in the lines

> O God, forasmuch as without Thee:
> We are not enabled to doubt Thee,
>   Pray, grant us Thy grace
>   To confess to Thy face
> We know nothing whatever about Thee.

He gave the impression that he was determined to succeed and more concerned to attain success than with the cause in whose name he attained it. The first mention in his *Diaries* of a real interest in deeper things comes in an entry of January 7, 1938, when he was preparing the Army Estimates. Warren Fisher called on him to discuss them, but, he records, 'instead of discussing the Estimates we talked about religion, philosophy and life after death.' (His opinions on this last topic were at this time very much those of my cynical Eton schoolmaster, Tuppy Headlam, who said 'Doubtless I shall inherit eternal bliss but I prefer not to contemplate so melancholy a proposition.) 'I told him that I had stayed', he continued, 'for a few days at Christmas with the nuns who had nursed my mother at Esperance in Eastbourne. He gave me *Verba Christi* and I sent him Renan's *La Vie de Jésus*!'

Later, at the time of his dismissal from the War Office when Chamberlain invited him to become President of the Board of Trade in its place and many were anxious that he should accept the office, he refused, saying that at the time of his mother's death he had overcome all ambition and had hesitated 'whether to continue in politics or occupy myself in more spirituality'.

If he ever felt seriously the temptation to absent himself from politics it was a temptation that he rejected. Nevertheless in all his closing years religious matters played a large part in his life, even to the extent of embarrassing by his preoccupation some of those with whom he had to associate. It so happened that the little town of Pewsey was in my constituency and, one evening when dining with him, I chanced to mention its name. Oddly enough he had never heard of the town of Pewsey but at once assumed that it was the home of Dr Pusey of the Oxford Movement, and gave me a long talk on that ecclesiastic, in whom I do not think that his other more political guests were especially interested. He lived on Wimbledon Common and among his neighbours there was Archbishop Godfrey, then the Apostolic Delegate, afterwards Archbishop of Liverpool and later of Westminster and Cardinal. In Belisha's depression after the catastrophe of Dunkirk they made friends and used to go for walks together on the Common. At Archbishop Godfrey's suggestion Belisha developed the habit of going into monastic retreat. He went to the Cistercian house of Mount St Bernard in Charnwood Forest and afterwards to St Michael's Abbey at Farnborough. In the habit that was then, and perhaps still is, all too common among certain naïve Catholics there is always, whenever a person of some public fame indulges in such activities, intense speculation that he is about to become a Catholic. There was a good deal of such speculation about Belisha and when he died *The Tablet* published a not very fortunate article of criticism, suggesting that he was an exhibitionist who was never seriously interested in the religious adventure. The article was much resented by certain of Belisha's friends and *The Tablet* had to apologise for it.

The truth is not easy to come by. It is certain that Belisha in his later years was a very different person from the flamboyant young man that we had known at Oxford in the 1920's. The failure at Dunkirk and his dismissal from the War Office had taught him that glittering distinctions and ambitious prizes were not likely to be easily attained and also that there was a vanity in the life that was wholly devoted to their attainment. Like King Lear his maturer taste demanded that he should meditate on the 'mystery of things' and nowhere was such meditation less easily come by than in the hurly-burly of politics, nowhere more easily than in a monastery. He did not wholly abandon politics. From time to time right up to the end and even when it had begun to appear very improbable that he would ever again climb to the top, he would at times complain that the world had treated him very unjustly, though indeed it was notable that he never uttered any word of complaint against any of the individuals who had been obstacles to his achievement. Yet to the last he would sometimes say that his day was yet to come. Yet he returned to the monastery and there he mixed, so far as it was possible, in the monastic life. He had no capacity for manual tasks—could not shave himself or pack a suitcase—and therefore, though he watched the monks at their work, such as weaving cloth or binding manuscripts, he was not able very usefully to assist them. Yet he joined with them in such simple tasks as he could—such as shocking corn. He read spiritual books—the Gospels and in particular Gerard Manley Hopkins, to whom he was most deeply devoted.

> The world is charged with the grandeur of God.
>    It will flame out, like shining from shook foil,
>    It gathers to a greatness like the ooze of oil
> Crushed. Why do men then now not reck his rod?
> Generations have trod, have trod, have trod;
>    And all is seared with trade; bleared, smeared with toil;
>    And wears man's smudge and shares man's smell: the soil
> Is bare now, nor can foot feel, being shod—

he quoted from Hopkins's *God's Grandeur* to Father Heath Robinson, Prior of Farnborough and son of the famous humorous artist, a little to that clergyman's surprise. How frequently he assisted at their services, how much he attended the Sacraments, how much he prayed, I cannot say. It may seem strange to compare Belisha to Ruskin, but I fancy that the saying of Dean Inge and G. K. Chesterton that Ruskin knew the use of everything in a church except the altar was not altogether inapplicable to Belisha.

At Farnborough Belisha derived pleasure from association with a critical master of such whimsical and eccentric mockery of the follies of the world as Father Robinson. But he took a bottle of whisky and a radio with him which he erected in his room and to which he appealed for assistance in his contemplation of the vanities of the world. I do not know that he ever expressed any ambition actually to become a Catholic. What he liked was the monastic life and it is not, I think, unfair to say that he appreciated the life more than the purpose of the life. He never had any ambition to be received by the well-bred Catholic aristocracy or to join those wealthy societies of men and women of whom Belloc so bitterly said that 'they enjoyed dining at Claridge's and talking about the sufferings of Christ'. Yet it is interesting that, even though he never deeply considered becoming a Catholic, it was almost exclusively among Catholics that he sought his religious company. I never heard of his taking any especial interest in the tenets of any other religion than the Christian—certainly not in the Jewish, to whose faith he had in a manner been brought up in the Jewish house at Clifton, but to whose orthodox practices he never adhered. He was of course hostile to anti-semitism—that was only natural—particularly at the time of *Truth*'s attack on him at his dismissal from the War Office largely because of his Jewish origins, but he never seemed to have any especial interest in the Zionist experiment. He was more Jewed against than Jewing. We may deduce from his frequent reading of the Bible that the example of Our Lord had come to be of very great significance to him. Is it fanciful to deduce from the fact that he gave Warren Fisher Renan's *Life of Jesus* that it was the general inspiration of Christian teaching rather than the historical claims by which he was especially attracted? Did there remain with him a tinge of doubt in his search after the ultimate mysteries? Something of the spirit in which fifty years ago he had written in the *Oxford Outlook*, 'In truth we were all ill at ease in the Zion of our long-ing.' When all was explored, did he finally feel that 'There are more things in heaven and earth, Horatio'?

# R. C. Robertson-Glasgow

'Flannelled fools at the wicket'
*The Islanders*—Rudyard Kipling

In spite of the disapproval of Mark Pattison and the Victorian Dons, games, and more particularly organised games, greatly increased in their prestige in the Oxford of the years immediately before the war. Undergraduates and Dons were still indeed content very often to take their exercise by going for immense walks, seeking perhaps to retrace the paths of *The Scholar Gipsy*, and, indeed, walks continued to be a feature of the Oxford of the 1920's, still comparatively uninvaded by the motor car. But organised sport was by then an important part of the undergraduate's life in which even the unathletic were expected to take an interest. Of the conflicts between Oxford and Cambridge by far the most important were the Boat Race and the cricket match.

The prestige of the University Boat Race, so early established and to this day so strangely maintained, was most peculiar. Only a very small proportion of the population knows anything about rowing or takes any interest in any other boat race except that between Oxford and Cambridge. Even among undergraduates only a very small proportion of them actually row. It is commonly—and truly—said that rowing is the only sport in which from beginning to end the participant continues to make always the same stroke. To be a rowing man is notoriously to submit oneself to a hard discipline which few consider sufficiently repaid by the slightly more generous diet provided while one is in training or by the opportunity for getting drunk at the bump-supper in the event of victory—the more so since even those who have never touched an oar or perhaps even approached the river are allowed to get every bit as drunk as the most stalwart stroke. Colleges are far more generous in

their financial support of the rowing club than of any other athletic
activities. It is generally believed—and I expect with justification—that
rowing is very bad for the health, that very many oarsmen strain their
hearts and die prematurely or at least sink into decrepitude. Maurice
Bowra used to complain that he had fought a world war in vain since it
had not even led to the abolition of rowing. Yet over the country,
readers of the newspapers and gogglers at the television box who have
never been to Oxford or Cambridge follow every detail of the race,
become vigorous champions of the one side or the other and are able
to pronounce that last year Oxford (or more probably Cambridge) won
the Boat Race, when they could not tell us on even the next day who was
the victor in any other University contest. And in spite of the increased
publicity which the media give in these days to so many other new
sports and contests and from which the traditional games are alleged so
greatly to suffer, there seems no abatement in the public interest in the
University Boat Race. It is strange and I do not know the explana-
tion.

How different is the story of cricket. In the years before the First War
cricket had established itself as the predominant English game. It was
cricket to which Mark Pattison particularly objected on account of the
inordinate time that it took—time which in the Rector of Lincoln's
opinion should properly be devoted to study. He himself was an adept
both at lawn tennis and at croquet—which, taking as they did so much
less time, he thought more suitable as the pastimes of educated gentlemen. But in spite of his hostility cricket established itself both in England
in general and in the Universities in particular as the game for Englishmen. Football was not yet formally differentiated into its codes. Golf,
until it was taken up by Mr Balfour, was not considered a serious University activity. There were, from the earliest times, and even before the
establishment of the County Championship, professionals who came
from the working classes yet were considered as licensed eccentrics to be
honoured for their skill at cricket. Wealthy and athletic amateurs balanced
half crowns on their stumps and offered them to the professional who
could bowl them down. Even such counties as Yorkshire which in the
years before the war fielded ten professionals in their team never dreamed
of not including one amateur to be their captain. At that time the notion
of an England that had not an amateur as its captain was unthinkable.
Lord Hawke expressed his heart-felt hope that he would never live to see
so dreadful a day. In that atmosphere, when the county fixture lists were
less crowded than they are today, when society contained many more

young men of independent income who could afford to devote their whole summers to cricket, when the social superiority of amateur to professional was not questioned, when the amateur was invited to play for his county if it was convenient but told that if on the day it proved inconvenient, there would be a professional on the ground who could be included to make up the team, when amateur and professional emerged on the ground from the pavilion through different gates, at Oxford the undergraduate who wished to devote himself to games and who was of sufficient capacity to win a Blue could content himself with a pass degree if indeed he even bothered with that. A story is told of Sammy Woods at Cambridge. He was persuaded against his better judgment to go in to a final tripos exam. Finding no question which in any way corresponded to anything within the limits of his knowledge he contented himself by writing 'Dam' on the paper and walking out. The kindly Dons said that they would have given him a pass degree if only he had been able to spell it right!

Cricket itself was by then a much less sophisticated game than it is today. Such techniques as the placing of the field, now so meticulously studied, were then left comparatively to chance. Amateur players were—at least many of them—somewhat carefree and had none of the anxiety of the professional as to whether they would be re-engaged for the next season.

The freedom from care of the pre-war amateur, though it has a degree of truth, is indeed often exaggerated. It is customary to ascribe the decline of light-hearted cricket entirely to the passing of the amateur and his ways of easy sportsmanship. I do not know that this is wholly true. There was no trick of gamesmanship in which Lord Frederick Beauclerk, ordained clergyman as he was, or W. G. Grace in a later age was not prepared to indulge, and doubtless no publicly confessed professional of his day who made as much money out of cricket as did W.G. 'A cheat on and off the field. . . . He exhibited extreme meanness and—oddest of all—physical cowardice,' C. P. Snow has written of Grace in his *Casebook of Sherlock Holmes*. He was an intermittent practitioner of medicine, his brother E. M. Grace a coroner. Between them, I once heard H. D. G. Leveson-Gower say, 'I think they made a very pretty business out of it.' Yet W.G. was a national figure as no one has been able to make himself in later days and when on the outbreak of the war he was persuaded to write a letter saying that winning the war was now more important than cricket, it was by many thought to be a strange and paradoxical opinion.

W. G. Grace
Had hair all over his face.
Lord, how the people cheered
When the ball got lost in his beard!

Even in post-war days it was not any professional but the Wykeham-ist Oxonian amateur Douglas Jardine who compelled his bowlers to resort to body-line as the only hope of mastering the menace of Bradman. 'That'll suit me fine. I'll knock the bugger's block off,' answered the fast bowler when Jardine gave him his instructions on the tactics he was to pursue.

In the pre-war world the Universities were allowed to rank as first class in their matches with the counties and were often fully equal to them. Players who had got their Blue could usually, if they wished, when the University term was ended, find a place in the county team of their residence. The Universities claimed and were freely accorded the right to play matches against Australian touring teams, and in 1878 Edward Lyttelton's famous Cambridge team actually defeated the full Australian eleven.

All this has greatly changed today and the reason for the change we will attempt to analyse a little later on. But what is important to note is that it did not change immediately after the war. Immediately after the war it was the ambition of those who remembered the halcyon days before 1914 as far as possible to restore everything exactly as it had been. The County Championship had of course come to an end during the war. It was restored immediately after it and with it the invariable amateur as a captain of all county teams. To begin with, it is true, the experiment was tried of giving only two days instead of the previous three for a county match, but that was found not to be at all a success and was immediately abandoned. Three-day matches came back both between the counties, and between Oxford and Cambridge and the counties in the Parks and at Fenner's. The distinctions between amateurs and profes-sionals were restored—not indeed quite in every offensive detail but essentially as they had previously been. The professionals in obedience to growing class consciousness were beginning a little to assert them-selves. The professional was no longer ready to touch his cap to the amateur in quite the old spirit. Formal and visible distinctions on the field or of entry on to the field were on the whole abolished, but 'off the field', wrote Cecil Parkin, the famous Lancashire bowler of the day, 'the professional frankly prefers to be left to himself.'

Yet cricket had still its prestige as the chief and most English of games. We were glad that Indians and West Indians had learnt it from us. It had never occurred to us that the day could possibly come when they would play it better than we did. At Oxford it was honoured alike by under-graduates—even those who did not themselves play—and by Dons and in those years immediately after the war Oxford and Cambridge between them produced eight English cricketers of whom four became captains of England teams. The four captains were A. E. R. Gilligan, A. P. F. Chapman, Douglas Jardine and G. O. Allen. The four other England players were G. E. C. Wood, J. C. W. McBryan, G. T. S. Stevens and C. S. Marriott. Even in more recent years the Universities have often given England their captains in Peter May, Ted Dexter and Colin Cowdrey, but the modern cricketer, even the most adept, who had had a University career, tends not to remain very long in first-class cricket. And in modern years the great characters have been less common since the abolition of the distinction between amateur and professional, with the severer programmes and the addition of so many one-day to the three-day matches. Today all players are professionals and even if amateurism had survived there are few who could have afforded to play as amateurs with any regularity. The professionals are concerned with keeping their place in the team and ensuring their re-engagement for the next season. They do not therefore take kindly to casual changes in the team or to an undergraduate in his Oxford vacation being put into it for a match or two in their place.

Nor, it must be confessed, is University cricket today by any means what it used to be. There are so many alternative sports and activities. Undergraduates play games less and, if they play cricket at all, fewer are willing to submit themselves to the discipline of playing it with the seriousness that is required to get them into the first class. Colleges have their Erratic and Eccentric teams, composed of those who do not even aspire to their regular College elevens, and who travel round the neigh-bouring villages, light-heartedly refreshing themselves after the match with copious pints at the village pub and are on the whole more popular than serious teams. Their opponents often do not well understand exactly who they are but are glad enough to welcome them. When my son was at Trinity, he brought down such a team, the Trinity Triflers, to play against our local team at Mells. Judging from the name of Trinity in their title, the villagers imagined that they would prove to be an eleven of clergymen. 'They be all old passons,' they explained. It turned out to be far from true.

As a consequence the Universities' matches against the counties are by no means what they were. They still indeed play against as many counties as in the past but the counties no longer trouble to send against them their full teams but take the opportunity to give a trial to some promising but unfledged young player. The Universities no longer keep a regular professional coach. Visiting teams from overseas are no longer willing to spare six days to play two three-day matches against the two Universities, but only play one match against a joint Oxford and Cambridge team. In the days before and immediately after the war the Oxford and Cambridge and the Eton and Harrow matches were the culmination of the London Season. People dressed themselves up in their smartest morning clothes and attended luncheon parties and teas of strawberries and cream offered in the various coaches that surrounded the ground. Enthusiastic cricketers actually watched the play. The more socially-minded circulated around behind the stands and indulged in gossip with their acquaintances. (I remember well how at the age of six I read in the paper of a particularly brilliant catch that had been made by the Oxford captain. I demanded of a young man whom I knew and who had been at the match that he give me a description of the feat and was quite horrified when he confessed that although indeed he had been at Lords throughout the match he had not at the moment been watching the cricket.) Today the University match, though it still takes place at Lords, is a sadly diminished affair. Those who go to it, whether for the cricket or for the social entertainment, are very many fewer and the game arouses so little interest that the question is constantly being raised whether there is any purpose in continuing to allow it to be held at Lords. Its continuing lack of popularity is in strange and sad contrast to the popularity of the Boat Race.

I was the most moderate of cricketers and never rose to any greater height than that of the Captain of the second match, Second Upper Club, at Eton—an honour which brought me the distinction of wearing, and at the end of the season distributing to others, the striped red cap which was known as the strawberry mess. But I had in youth, and still have in old age, a great passion for following the game. My meticulous attention to the county scores brought down on me during my undergraduate career considerable criticism from my intellectual and aesthetic friends who insisted on regarding so bourgeois and eccentric a taste as no more than a pose. My most notable, though not perhaps most creditable, performance on the cricket field was at the age of 12, when I was in the eleven of my preparatory school at Summer Fields down the Banbury Road in North Oxford. We had to play against Horris Hill at Newbury.

Up till then we had that season remained unbeaten, but it was well known that Horris Hill's team was greatly stronger than ours. The master who was in charge of our games therefore devised the plan that if we won the toss we should bat all day and thus make a draw of the match. So it worked out. The earlier batsmen did their best to obey their ignoble orders and remained at the crease each as long as they could. Yet wickets steadily fell. I was in No 8. As a general rule I was the most impatient of batsmen. I hit out wildly, usually succumbing to a very early ball and, if my luck happened to be in, making a few but making them very quickly. This day, however, I very well understood that my duty was different. I stayed there for about two hours and made 18, only enlivened by one hit to leg for four off the bowling of Douglas Jardine. Thus was the match drawn and our faith unfaithful kept falsely true. A member of the Horris Hill eleven who was afterwards a fellow colleger at Eton told me how when stumps were drawn he felt gravely tempted to pick up the ball and throw it at me. The match was uniquely remarkable for me because it was the only time in which I played with two subsequent captains of England, G. O. Allen for Summer Fields and Douglas Jardine for Horris Hill.

Some fifty years after this Summer Fields–Horris Hill match I met Douglas Jardine over a cocktail and reminded him of it. Much water had flowed under the bridges in between—two wars and in the world of cricket the body-line controversy over which he had presided. Yet I found that he vividly remembered this match at Summer Fields in the summer of 1914 and still bitterly resented the unsporting conduct in it of Mr Alington our cricket master. He remembered also my innings but did not so deeply resent—or at any rate pretended that he did not so deeply resent—that thinking truly enough that I was no more than a robot obeying like a slave my master's voice with which I was too craven to interfere. Soon after he was dead, unforgiving no doubt of Mr Alington to the last.

Jardine was about my age—I fancy, just a few months older—and was up at Oxford in the 1920's of which I write, at the same time as I. I used to meet him from time to time in the rooms of Philip Landon, who was the Bursar of Trinity. Landon liked to collect around him the notables of the University—athletic or otherwise. He boasted that he had denied himself matrimony for his love of Oxford and had devoted himself to 'begetting the idea'. What idea exactly it was not very easy to see. Jardine was sometimes in his rooms. I met him there but made no pretence to have got to know him well. The two first-class cricketers who figured most largely in my life were C. B. Fry and Crusoe Robertson-Glasgow. C. B. Fry was of course a great deal older than I and was indeed, to begin with, a companion of my father and my uncle, who had both been with him at Repton. My father was slightly his senior, my uncle his exact contemporary. My uncle was a man of no particular distinction—whether academic or athletic—but Fry, who was a generous man, liked to have something kindly to say about anyone of his acquaintance. He liked my uncle, but when I asked him for any word of commendation on his achievements all that he could think to say was, 'He used to sit at the back of the class and, when the master was not looking, make a noise like a cow.' Then he added meditatively, 'He was very good at making a noise like a cow.'

As a general rule the fame of great athletes is, like that of most other public persons, extremely fleeting. In the day of their achievement their name is upon every lip. Then they retire and are soon forgotten. Fry's achievement was so wholly out of the ordinary that he remained to the end a public figure. My father remembered having seen him make the world's record long jump and never forgot it. Fry would certainly have won the world's long jump at the Olympic Games, but he did not enter for the competition. When they asked him why, he said that he had not heard that they were going on. He came into my life in the early 1920's when he stood as Liberal candidate for Banbury. Then a year later when Frank Gray, the Liberal Member, had been unseated on petition because of the blunders of his agent Fry stood in the by-election as the Liberal candidate for Oxford. On both occasions he was defeated. He was not a conventionally well-informed candidate. He had his own technique. They asked him 'Why was there unemployment in England but none in France?' He replied gaily. 'I have no idea—no idea whatsoever, bowled me middle stump—neck and crop. By the way what does neck and crop mean?' They cheered him to the echo as lustily as if he had given a properly considered answer. Later he stood for Brighton but there also he was beaten and in closing years became very critical of Liberals whom he considered—rightly enough—to be in a general way unathletic and indifferent to the rhythm and proper balance of ball-room dancing on which the well-being of the soul, he had by then come to learn, was primarily dependent. I met him during these last years through Douglas Jerrold and when we formed out little publishing house of Hollis and Carter he came on our board. He was the most genial and kindly of colleagues but it would be idle to pretend that he was a regular attendant at the office—there was no reason why he should have been—or that at board meetings his remarks confined themselves very strictly to the agenda nominally under discussion. He preferred rather to tell how he had been offered the throne of Albania but refused it or how when he represented Ranjitsinjhi at the League of Nations a rival Indian prince gave him poison which was calculated to unhinge his mind—two anecdotes which I frequently heard but never wholly believed.

His wife looked after all his financial affairs and was of great service to him. When she died I wrote him a letter of condolence. He replied, 'Dear Christopher, It is quite all right,' and went on to complain about his income tax. We once dined together at Brown's Hotel, which he much frequented. As we sat after the meal in the lounge there was an elderly gentleman who inserted himself into our conversation. As a result, when a round of drinks was ordered he was included in it and when it came to Fry's turn to order the round he again included the interlocutor. The old gentleman was so abundantly treated that before the evening was out he had collapsed and had to be helped, unconscious, to the lavatory. 'Who is this old man?' I asked Fry as we laid him out. 'I've no idea,' he said. 'I thought he was a friend of yours.' Each had regaled him under the impression that he was a friend of the other. It was only in incapacity that we discovered that he was a mere gate-crasher. 'Twelfth man's benefit,' commented Fry. 'First time I ever heard of a twelfth man retired hurt.'

More frequently than Jardine of New College to be found in Landon's rooms was Lionel Hedges who was an undergraduate at Trinity itself. Lionel Hedges had come up from Tonbridge with a tremendous reputation as a schoolboy cricketer, having already played for Kent. He was a master of parlour tricks but had no great academic talents. A seedy-looking middle-aged gentleman called on him one morning of a match. Imagining him to be a reporter, Lionel said to him brusquely, 'I have nothing to say to you.' The man tried to expostulate but Lionel repeated, 'I have nothing to say to you.' It only afterwards transpired that the seedy man was not a reporter but his tutor, with whom he was not otherwise acquainted. It was only with the greatest difficulty that he somehow or other scraped through any examinations and it was with almost greater difficulty that he evaded urgent financial crises. Yet he was always ready with a bright anecdote. His cricketing prowess was such that they gladly took him as a master at Cheltenham 'for his muscular rather than his mental qualities', as Lord Birkenhead once said of a certain Bishop with whom he had quarrelled, and he played there a number of times for Gloucestershire.

To everyone's sorrow he died in 1934 at the age of 30. Cecil Day Lewis, who was afterwards to be Poet Laureate, celebrated his noble batsmanship in a triumphantly laudatory ode.

It was also with Landon that I met Robertson-Glasgow. I had first come across his name in connection with the Eton and Charterhouse cricket match of 1918. It had been the arrogant habit of Eton before the war to play inter-school matches only with Harrow and Winchester— Harrow at Lords and Winchester alternately at Winchester and Eton. The war of course interrupted those habits. The Harrow match was no longer played at Lords and both the Harrow and Winchester matches were reduced from two days to one. In this extremity Eton consented to enlarge their list and a match was arranged with Charterhouse. Crusoe Robertson-Glasgow was at the time a Carthusian and was a member of their team. I noted his peculiar name and it remained with me. The match was entirely a disaster for the Carthusians. Batting against Basil Hill Wood and A. G. Gore, Charterhouse were shot out for 13. Robertson-Glasgow who opened their innings was given out for o caught at the wicket, as he alleged on returning to the pavilion, 'off his top button'.—'Not that it matters,' he gaily said. Eton in reply did not for a time do much better and six wickets were down for 21, but recovering, they eventually managed 168.

It was as a bowler of course that Robertson-Glasgow won his place in first-class teams, though he could also blossom out as a batsman, but was firmly warned off any ambitions in that direction by Frank Gilligan, his Oxford captain, and afterwards by John Daniell from Somerset. He was told that his physique was not such that he could safely become an all-rounder, and this was undoubtedly true. It is sometimes said that the intense application to the passage and behaviour of a small leather ball is not good for the development of other mental capacities and that first-class cricketers are not in general a very brainy lot. It would obviously be easy enough to find examples of this truth. 'Never read print,' said W. G. Grace. 'It spoils you for seeing the ball.' But there are others for whom the law is not true. C. B. Fry, for instance, was a brilliant classical scholar who was prevented by a mental breakdown from success in his schools but whom nobody, I fancy, would ever be so foolish as to call a fool. It was the same with Robertson-Glasgow. He worked by fits and starts, lacking steady application. He, too, suffered from instability in his mind, which caused a number of breakdowns.

He had been a scholar at Charterhouse and went up as a scholar to Corpus Christi College, Oxford. He loved the traditional, central

English poetry—the poetry of rhyme and metre—particularly Keats. For modernisms, whether in poetry or in life, he had no liking. He was a strong conservative and was led by his conservatism to champion strongly the claims of a classical education, despising all modernistic substitutes. He had a liking for writing Greek and Latin verse which, as a student of Mods, he studied at Corpus under the tutorship of Richard Livingstone, the author of *A Defence of Classical Education*. Livingstone found his verse uneven but detected high virtue in occasional lines as when he translated:

> O, gloomy lands and fast decaying realms

as:      A, populos tristes et tabescentia regna,

which Livingstone praised as 'the best line that he had been offered that term'.

Robertson-Glasgow had come up to Oxford with two aims—to get a cricket Blue and a good degree. But, though encouraged by Livingstone, he soon found cricket more demanding than Latin verse. He satisfied himself with a moderate class in Mods and, going on to Greats, was quite horrified by metaphysical problems of Appearance and Reality and soon had no intentions in that direction but to scrape through with a pass of some sort—which he just managed to achieve.

He was quite without ambition for a career. During his school days he won a number of prizes for essays by dint of assiduously cramming up the requisite matter, but, far from being proud of the achievement, was very deeply ashamed of it and considered it as pot-boiling, of which no honourable man would have been guilty. 'A taste for the public service ... not promptly checked', he wrote, 'has begun to sap men's manhood. There is no passion more debilitating to the mind, unless perhaps it be that itch of public speaking which it not infrequently begets.'

In his post-Oxford life Robertson-Glasgow was content to be a preparatory school master and then held various ephemeral journalistic jobs and did some amusing cricket broadcasts, delighting the public on one occasion by explaining the antics of a dog which ran across the pitch at a test match. He wrote most entertainingly and Prendergast, it will be remembered in Sir John Masterman's *To Teach the Senators Wisdom* selected him and Neville Cardus as the two supreme masters of modern episodic English prose. But he never showed much desire to bind himself to a steady job. He had a great contempt for sycophancy. A worshipping henchman described how he was privileged to take a ride on horse back with his master, Lord Beaverbrook. 'There we were,' he said, 'the

Chief ahead and me just behind, just like Napoleon and Marshal Ney.' 'Marshal Yea, surely,' said Crusoe.

His favourite form of conversation in his undergraduate days was the relation of anecdotes of the great figures of pre-1914 cricket. I remember in particular two. One was of F. S. Jackson who was captaining a team against the Australians at Headingley. He was proposing to bowl himself, when a stentorian spectator shouted out, 'Take yerself off. Put on Schofield.' (Schofield Haig was the then very popular Yorkshire professional.) Jackson took no notice and proceeded to bowl an over in which he took four Australian wickets. When they got back to the pavilion, the spectator came on to him and said, 'It were I who told you to take yerself off, Mr Jackson.' 'Well, you spoke a little out of turn, didn't you?' said Jackson. 'Eh, but, Mr Jackson, they batted bad—they batted bad,' said the man with typical Yorkshire refusal to make any concession.

The other was of a match between Leicestershire and Nottingham at Leicester. In those harder days professionals did not get generous hotel accommodation when they played away. They had to do the best that they could. Leicestershire had at that time a very good but very pious batsman called Knight, Nottinghamshire had a less inhibited bowler called Wass. When the Nottingham team arrived at Leicester Knight offered Wass hospitality but since he did not have a spare bedroom Wass had to be accommodated behind a hastily erected curtain which was made to divide the room. As soon as they had got to bed Wass heard Knight beseeching the Almighty that of His infinite goodness He would on the next day allow Knight to score a century off Wass. Wass was not going to stand for this, and in a louder voice sent up a counter-petition that on the contrary on the next day he would be permitted to 'get that bugger Knight for a duck'.

'And what happened?' I asked Crusoe.

'Why, God did the only thing that any decent God who wanted to preserve a relic of self-respect could possibly have done,' he said. 'The next morning when they got up they found the rain fairly teeming down. The wicket was under water, and so it continued for three days. The match was abandoned without a ball being bowled.'

His main ambition, as he confessed on going up to Oxford, was to get a cricket Blue. That of course he achieved. He got it as a freshman in 1920—which was incidentally before I came up to Oxford and before I met him—when the Oxford and Cambridge match was spoiled by rain and ended in a draw. In 1921 he played again and Cambridge won by an innings and 24 runs. 1922 was a lean year for him and he had some difficulty in holding his place. It was an even worse year for Oxford, and Cambridge beat them by an innings and 103 runs. But in 1923 he played again and Oxford reversed the fortunes, winning by an innings and 227. His four Varsity matches did not bring him great personal success. In all of them he only managed to take two wickets. Yet his bowling in the Parks attracted sufficient notice for John Daniell in 1920 to ask him to play for Somerset.

In 1924 just after he had left Oxford he was chosen to play for the Gentlemen against the Players having just got 9 for 38 for Somerset against Middlesex. Though he never played for England he felt justified in boasting—I have no doubt truly enough—that he was considered by the selectors for inclusion in the England team. He rightly thought this a high honour.

He went to Australia as reporter of an England tour. He had an admiration for high clowning and developed there something of a hero-worship for Patsy Hendren. Patsy Hendren used to field in the deep and won the favour of the crowd on the Hill at Sydney by replying to their jeers by saying, 'They're only playing the good lookers today!' Handsome looks were not Patsy's most notable feature but his repartee intensely pleased them and it was passed down from row to row in the Australian way. He had won them and every time that he fielded the ball they cheered him to the echo.

Prominent among his social pleasures Crusoe rated the playing of dab-cricket, particularly in the company of his great friend, Ben Travers, the dramatist. It is a game that preparatory schoolboys play or used to play. You draw out a squared line of paper with numbers and methods of dismissal—bowled, leg before wicket, caught, stumped and the like—on the squares. Then shutting your eyes, you proceed to dab with a pencil and credit the imaginary players with the fate which the dabbed pencils record for them. 'The moving finger writes and having writ.' It pleased his lively and in some ways perhaps infantile mind to play games by this method between imaginary teams. I remember a match of musicians against painters, and his joy when Beethoven, at the time partnering Mozart, was dabbed a 'run out'. He delighted in the concoction that Beethoven, owing to his deafness, had failed to hear Mozart's call and had consequently been caught stranded in the middle of the pitch.

Had it been so, his fate would not have been very different from that of Crusoe himself on a certain memorable and most ludicrous occasion. He was playing for Oxford at the Oval against Surrey and I chanced to have gone to watch the match. Crusoe batted at No 9. His partner was Tom Raikes, an old Wykehamist who was one of the players in that famous match between Summer Fields and Horris Hill of which I have already spoken. Crusoe played a ball to the deep field at the pavilion end, called for and safely took a run. Then, turning, he called for a second. Raikes began to obey his call, but, half-way down the pitch, decided that he could never make the further crease. He turned back to the wicket-keeper's end. But Crusoe was by that time in full career and was not to be reversed. He, too, continued on his scramble to the same end and they processed towards it side by side. Arrived there, they decided that all was not well and that at least one batsman should be at the bowler's end. But which? They both decided to make a dash for it and proceeded up the pitch together. Meanwhile the ball was returned to Strudwick, the wicket-keeper, who naturally removed the bails. The umpires were by then helpless with laughter. They had no hesitation in giving a verdict of Out. But who was out? That was much less easy to say but Raikes solved the dilemma by going to the pavilion. He had, as he afterwards said, left a pint standing on the bar there and thought it a pity that it should be kept waiting. Crusoe afterwards told me that Bill Hitch who was fielding at short-leg, said to him, 'You know who was really out, don't you?' 'No, I don't know and I doubt if anybody knows,' Crusoe replied. 'You was,' said Hitch in a sepulchral voice.

If this was his most absurd day at the Oval his finest day came some years later. It must be confessed that it had nothing to do with Oxford, but it so chanced that I was again there to see the feat. It was in 1926 and Crusoe was that day playing for Somerset against Surrey. The match had gone very decidedly Surrey's way and Somerest in the fourth innings had to make 402 to win. They did not look like coming near to making them. Wickets fell steadily and when the ninth wicket fell Somerset were still 217 behind. Robertson-Glasgow was the eleventh man. His partner was the most graceful of batsmen, P. R. Johnson, the inheritor of the mantle and all the driving grace and power of Lionel Palairet. Johnson had to earn his living and consequently was only able to play irregularly in county matches. But his irregular appearances were quite sufficient to earn him his reputation. He was invited to go to Australia with the team of P. F. Warner and J. W. H. T. Douglas but because of business was unable to accept the invitation. Always faultlessly dressed, it was his habit to drive up to a match arrayed in top hat and spotless morning coat. He would say to his fellow players, 'Just been doing a spot of work,' as he changed into his flannels. In those days when Sunday was *dies non* for cricketers whose match had begun on the Saturday and was to continue on the Monday and Tuesday he always spent his Sunday in bed reading Dickens. Now, as Crusoe came out, he stood there with a silk handkerchief knotted round his neck and greeted his partner with a welcoming smile. He then turned to the Surrey bowling and laid about it, especially favouring the rocketing drive that found the gap between mid-off and the bowler on its way to the boundary. Crusoe joined in and hit one six which bounced in the road that runs by the Oval and then lost itself in a neighbouring pub. The 200 went up. Then 250. Then 300. At first the Surrey professionals, thinking that the game was in the bag for them, showed sportsmanlike sympathy for the gallant losers. Then, as the total mounted through the 300's their sympathy gave way to anxiety and frustration. 'Why can't yer get yerself out?' they said to Crusoe. They had clearly lost all hope of getting Peter Johnson out. At last some time in the 320's Crusoe saw on the board that his own score was 49. With a rush to the head he chopped at a ball outside the off-stump, touched it and was caught at the wicket. Somerset thus lost its gallant fight by 77 runs. Johnson was 117 not out. He was 46 years old and this proved to be his last and grandest century in county cricket.

It may be wondered why Crusoe ever played for Somerset. He came from Aberdeenshire and had no reasonable connection with or qualification for Somerset. In the years before the war Somerset cricket was in a sad way. Somerset has none of the large towns which every other first-class county possesses. In the days before motor cars it was difficult to attract sufficient gates to make finances satisfactory. It was compelled therefore to rely, more than other counties, on amateurs, who, of course, could not play regularly because of the demands of earning a living. They therefore could not keep a regular team. John Daniell was their exuberant captain. It is said that he used to go down to the station at Bath and, posting himself by the collector who took the tickets of those who had come off the train, shout out, 'Anybody on this train play cricket?' If anyone answered 'Yes' he would say, 'You had better come along then and play for Somerset.' One can hardly believe this to be true. But it certainly is true, as he himself told me, that my friend B. D. Hylton-Stewart, afterwards Music Master at Marlborough and the organist of St James's, Piccadilly, went one day when shortly before the 1914 war he was an undergraduate at Cambridge down to the ground at Bath to be a spectator of a match. His father was a local vicar. Daniell, seeing him seated on one of the benches, said, 'We're one short. You had better get changed and make up the team.' When the match was all over, he said to the Somerset eleven in disgust. 'You're not a cricket team. You're a travelling circus.'

After the war when county cricket was resumed, for these various reasons and because, unlike so many other counties, it had no professional local leagues from which it could draw promising young players, there was no county whose prospects were more uncertain than those of Somerset. Yet Daniell was quite determined to put the county on its feet again and to do so unhesitatingly raided the Universities to recruit good amateur players. He got McBryan and M. D. Lyon, Bunty Longrigg, Lowry and Robertson-Glasgow. In the recruitment he paid no pedantic attention to the niceties of the qualification regulations by which any player before he played for a county was supposed to have been born there or to have resided there for two years. Tom Lowry of a distinguished New Zealand family was born at Wellington in that country. Daniell decided that this covered Wellington near Taunton in Somerset. Crusoe Robertson-Glasgow, as I have said, was born and brought up in Aberdeenshire, but he had a cousin who lived at Hinton Charterhouse outside Bath. This to Daniell was sufficient. It was from Somerset cricket that Robertson-Glasgow gained his peculiar nickname. One of the first games that he played for them was against Essex and the first wicket that he took was that of the great eccentric Essex batsman C. P. McGahey. When McGahey came back to the pavilion someone who had missed his dismissal asked him how he was out. 'Bowled neck and crop by a bugger called Robinson Crusoe,' said McGahey in much disgust.

He continued to bowl for Somerset and to entertain the Somerset crowd up till the 1930's. I remember him fielding in the deep on a sunny day at Weston-super-Mare and when a wicket fell making a dash for the refreshment tent. He was loudly applauded by the crowd when he returned as the next batsman came in.

Whatever the respective merits of rival games it is certain that cricket is the game that is best written about and the one about which it is best to read. It was only comparatively recently that the art of cricket-writing was developed. Victorian sports-reporting was an uninspiring affair. It has been my great good fortune to have enjoyed the friendship of a number of outstanding cricket writers—John Arlott, Alan Gibson, Ian Peebles and Jack Fingleton. But all of them would, I think, agree that the creator and first master of their art was Neville Cardus, who in these years of the early 1920's wrote his daily piece for the *Manchester Guardian* comparing the batting of Spooner to the music of Mozart or Woolley to something out of Wagner. Even before I came to Oxford I had already heard a good deal about Cardus in addition to my daily reading of him, for he had been during the war not only cricket coach at Shrewsbury but also for a time secretary to Dr Alington, who was then the Headmaster there and afterwards Headmaster of Eton. Alington made him his secretary because he found him one day at the nets while the new batsmen were buckling on their pads reading the poems of Walter de la Mare which he had brought with him in his pocket but Alington did not, it must be confessed, think very highly of Cardus's own cricketing prowess and used to tell how Cardus was the only man whom he had ever known who bowled a ball in one net which pitched and dismissed the batsman in the net next door.

In 1923, when Lancashire came up to play the University, Crusoe suggested that we should invite Cardus to dinner, which we most gladly did on the rest Sunday of the match. We invited him to dine with us at the George and bring with him whoever of the Lancashire team might wish to come. The Lancashire professionals did not, as a general rule, appreciate the finer points of musical appreciation and the critical words in which he sometimes described their cricketing exploits did not make him as popular with them as he was with the reading public. 'T' bloudy Cardus' they commonly called him, and the rest very reasonably preferred their own company with which they were familiar to that of unknown and to them alien friends. However, Cecil Parkin, who was an exact epitome of what Arnold Bennett would have called a card, was a man who had no such inhibitions. Cecil Parkin, perhaps not so well remembered today was, at that time, a public figure. He had just returned from the M.C.C. trip to Australia and entertained us with anecdotes which in these days would doubtless have found their way into some newspaper's gossip column but which in those more restrained times still remained firmly unpublished. He told us of his quarrels with P. G. H. Fender and the outcry of the Melbourne crowd against E. R. Wilson, who had indiscreetly published some criticisms of the Australian umpires in articles which he had sent home to English papers in those days when members of touring teams had not yet been forbidden to write articles. The crowd, Parkin told us, had risen against Wilson like animals and but for Parkin's gallant protection would have torn him limb from limb. I have never been content with the reading of the athletic exploits of great players but have always been curious to know anecdotes of their private escapades off the field, and the evening was a fascination to me. We asked Parkin of the rumour that was then current that Jack

Hobbs was a consumptive. 'Only at mealtimes,' he replied. He had a number of cynical anecdotes about the sums of money which certain prominent members of amateur status were making out of cricket.

Crusoe's last twenty years were spent in sadness due to the terrible fits of depression from which he had suffered ever since undergraduate days. His wife, who had also been his nurse, looked after him heroically. But he could not endure the sight of fields of blank snow and one day, when the landscape was so covered and there was no hint of a thaw, his mind gave and he took a fatal overdose of drugs.

# Evelyn Waugh

Proud and godly kings had built her, long ago,
With her towers and tombs and statues all arow,
With her fair and floral air and the love that lingers there,
And the streets where the great men go.
                    *The Dying Patriot*—James Elroy Flecker

I went up to Oxford, to Balliol, in October 1920. Evelyn Waugh was a year and a half behind me and did not arrive until January 1922 when he went to the smaller College of Hertford. We have from his own pen two accounts of his early life, *A Little Learning*, the first volume of what was to have been a full autobiography, and the private and much more outspoken *Diaries*, which he had never intended for publication. These *Diaries* were sold by his widow—now dead—and there is much controversy whether she and whether Evelyn's literary agent, A. D. Peters, also now dead, did right in making available for publication what Evelyn had never intended for any but his private eye. Certainly the picture of misery which he gives there is very different from the frank but on the whole genial, restrained and happy portrait of *A Little Learning*. (I cannot understand Dudley Carew's verdict that that is a bitter book.) At the time of my writing, the most excellent life of Evelyn Waugh by my friend, Christopher Sykes, had not yet been published, but he most kindly let me see a copy of his proofs, and I do not think that there is any material difference between our interpretations. There is in that book a deep and generous tribute to his kindly father, which one would never have surmised from the very critical entries in the *Diaries*. *A Little Learning* makes no attempt to conceal the liberal drinking of his Oxford days and indeed of his subsequent life, but they give no picture of the almost constant and unrestrained soaking which we might derive from the *Diaries*. Many of us who knew him very well would have been content, had the *Diaries* never been published, to conceal facts which we knew and to confine ourselves to such anecdotes as he had seen fit to give to the world. How many of us would be unashamed if all the facts of our life, particularly perhaps of our undergraduate life, were published to the world?

However that may be, the *Diaries* having been published, there is now no point in not discussing them frankly. Mr Anthony Powell in a notice of my *Seven Ages* in *The Daily Telegraph* says of me that 'I think it could truly be said that there was no friend to whom he [Evelyn Waugh] was more devoted throughout his life,' and Evelyn in *A Little Learning* wrote that 'Christopher Hollis became and has remained one of my closest friends.' Whether I quite deserve these extreme recommendations it is not for me to say, but certainly he was my most intimate companion during my closing terms at Oxford and certainly, as was his habit with his old friends, he preserved until death that friendship without a single of those episodes of misunderstanding by which his life with others was so often marred. He was often our guest at Stonyhurst. He was then our neighbour to the east at Stinchcombe in Gloucestershire and to the west at Combe Florey near Taunton. For a time after leaving Stinchcombe he planned to settle even nearer to us—at Nunney or at Batcombe, where we inspected a commodious house. It had a glassed verandah, and Evelyn, anxious to learn whether this verandah caught the morning sun, asked the old man who was showing us the house where the sun rose. "'E do rise in the east, 'e do,' explained the ancient of this curious Batcombe custom.

As Evelyn records, he had kept his diary, unknown to anybody but himself, during his earlier years, and he started keeping it again after he had gone down, during the years of depression which ended with his attempted suicide and during which he was a frequent visitor to Oxford, but he was too much engaged to keep it during his undergraduate time. There is therefore no record of his day-to-day adventures during those years. Yet the *Diaries* tell us enough for us to form a fairly complete picture of the sort of life that he would then have depicted himself as leading. He came up to Hertford in January 1922 and, as he himself tells us, during his first two terms lived a quiet and comparatively orderly life, dining regularly in Hall and consorting mainly with members of his own College and with old Lancing companions at New College. We in the outer world, so far as we were aware of him at all, knew only that the brother of Alec Waugh, the author of *The Loom of Youth*, which we had all read at school, had come up to Oxford. I do not know that I myself ever met him during those two terms.

It was with the Michaelmas term of 1922 that he first blossomed forth as a public figure in undergraduate life and that I first got to know him. Thenceforward we were constant companions. The two revelations in the *Diaries* by which those who consider it their duty to be shocked have been most shocked are the revelations of his homosexual habits and of his continual drunkenness. He has also of course been widely criticised for snobbery and for what is alleged to have been his sadistic bullying and unmeasured vituperation of those who incurred his disfavour—sometimes, it is said, people of small importance and without means to defend themselves—and of people who had never done him any great disservice.

How far were these revelations of himself true? The answer to that is that they were all undoubtedly true, but that they were by no means the whole of the truth. The confessions of the *Diaries* are confessions, if not by any means, in their earlier extracts, confessions of a reluctant penitent. He had certainly in those years at Oxford two very central homosexual affairs—with Richard Pares, whom he mentions by name in *A Little Learning*, and with Alastair Graham, who appears in the book under the pseudonym of 'Hamish Erskine'. I knew both of them very well. It was indeed in Richard Pares's room in Balliol that I first met Evelyn. He and Evelyn were not a well-assorted pair. Richard Pares was the son of Sir Bernard Pares, well known as an expert on Russian affairs. He was a scholar at Balliol from Winchester and in many ways a most typical Wykehamist. His natural company was with his books. He was fairly clearly destined to become a Don, and had indeed a distinguished scholastic career and became the learned historian of the West Indian sugar trade and a Professor of Edinburgh University. He would very probably have become the Master of Balliol had he not tragically been afflicted with a disease of paralysis from which he died. He was of floppy light hair and good looking and attracted, as such young men did, the attention of Sligger Urquhart, the Dean of Balliol, who christened him Wig. It would not have been at all natural for him to waste his time in dissipation, but Evelyn's personal dominance was powerful. He made strong demands on those to whom he offered affection—they must do as he did—and in particular the demand to join with him in the bouts of heavy drinking which he had at that time erected almost into an article of religion. Richard obeyed him for a time, but the exercise was not natural to him. Indeed he was not physically capable of drinking glass for glass with Evelyn, and after a few such experiments and a not very convincing pretence of endorsing the cause of insobriety as a worthy manlike cause—he even made a speech at the Union in favour of drunkenness—the incompatibility was too obviously great, and he and Evelyn came to recognise that they were men of different habits. 'Richard, you're not a great man, and I'm not a great man, but John's a great man and he's in distress,' Evelyn reported of their great friend, John Sutro, as Sutro sprawled uncontrollably drunk in an armchair, inert as a sack of potatoes and had in the end to be conveyed back to his College of Trinity in a wheelbarrow. Evelyn and Richard Pares drifted apart, though there was never anything at all of the nature of a quarrel between them.

Alastair Graham, with whom he picked up about a year later, was of a very different nature. He was the son of a wealthy father, by then dead, and of a mother who came from the American South and was a few years later to be depicted as the dominating Lady Circumference in *Decline and Fall*. Alastair was quite without ambition or any academic qualifications. He failed in all the necessary examinations and was duly sent down from Oxford. His mother was greatly concerned at his progress or lack of it and after his Oxford dismissal she obtained entry for him to an architectural school in London but was greatly concerned later to discover that he in fact never attended its classes. He spent all his time at Oxford where he went about from drinking party to drinking party with Evelyn. He had more money than Evelyn or any of the rest of us, and indeed possessed a car to which none of the rest of us dreamed of aspiring. It was a two-seater, which accommodated a third passenger in its dicky. Claud Cockburn, Evelyn's cousin and today a well-known ex-Communist and contributor to *Private Eye* and other such satirical papers, then a nervous young Liberal, used often to ride as this third passenger. He was able so to curl himself up that he could comfortably shut up the lid and thus protect himself against the rain. When I was President of the Union I put Claud on the paper to speak in a debate against Imperial Preference. He was so nervous that at dinner, to which I entertained him along with the other speakers, he was hardly able to hold his glass for shaking—a disability from which he has never after- wards, I think, been found to suffer!

Mrs Graham, Alastair's mother—Mrs G as we called her—was, as I say, frankly disturbed at the habits into which Alastair was falling, but— quite wrongly—held me much more responsible for them than Evelyn. One day when I was staying at their house at Barford in Warwickshire,

Alastair refused to leave the dinner-table after the meal was finished but insisted, in spite of his mother's protest, on staying there drinking. Eventually Mrs Graham demanded that I should leave the table and come to talk to her. Alastair begged me to pay no attention to his mother's command, but, as a guest, I felt that I had no alternative but to obey. She gave me a lecture. She explained how concerned she was about Alastair's conduct. Her promise to her dying husband had been to care for her boy's welfare, and she could not but be distressed at the way he was turning out. For his misdemeanours I was more responsible than Evelyn or any other of his undesirable friends. 'For of course you're so much older.' This was not to any significant extent true, but it was an impression that she had formed and with her impressions once formed could never be either removed or substantiated.

Yet, in spite of such disapproval she always remained most kindly to me and, disapproving as she was of our constant excursions to pubs and other such undesirable destinations, I was always welcome to her house. I was very fond of Alastair as were all of his friends, but I was always puzzled by her conviction that I was the cause of his misdoings. For I knew well that I was a fairly constant and well-accepted companion but I had no influence over him at all. It was only a year or two afterwards that I found out the cause of her prejudice. She was, as I say, of a high family—'a lovely family', as she called it—from the Southern United States and I found that she was convinced from the thickness of my lips that I had black blood in me. As she one day confided to Evelyn, 'I've not lived in the Southern States for nothing.' I have come across from time to time others who have formed a similar impression. I could not have had the smallest objection were it so. I am the inheritor, like most people, of a good deal of mixed blood, but it comes from Eastern Europe, not from across the Atlantic. Indeed I have never heard of any member of my family before my generation who has ever crossed the Atlantic, still less been to Africa. So I do not see how her impression can have been true.

For a time Alastair toyed with the notion of going into the neighbouring Stratford-on-Avon to learn printing from Bernard Newdigate, but I do not think that he ever actually went or, as far as I know, did any other work of any sort. Our habit was as I say to drive around the country from pub to pub and our conversation mainly consisted in commenting with approval on any acquaintance or any whom we met who displayed any sort of eccentricity as 'a zany'—which we considered to be a mark of very high approval.

During his closing time at Oxford and for a few years afterwards Evelyn and Alastair were almost constantly in one another's company—a companionship which is to some extent described in the companionship of Ryder and Sebastian Flyte in *Brideshead Revisited*. Then for some reason which I have never been able to discover Alastair faded out of Evelyn's life—out of Evelyn's and mine and that of all our friends. He did not go like Sebastian to Tunis, but he went to Greece. However, he did not remain there, but returned to this country, where he went to live and from all accounts still lives in a house somewhere in South Wales. I last saw him when my wife and I visited the house of Edward Longford, brother of the present Lord Longford, near Mullingar in Central Ireland in 1930. Evelyn was a fellow guest, as incidentally was John Betjeman. I have heard from Billy Clonmore, now the Earl of Wicklow, who now lives near Dun Laoghaire, that he once visited and was seen in Dublin. Otherwise I have never heard of anyone who has seen him for many years. Evelyn, as I say, certainly never saw him during those years, and this was a curiosity. For in general Evelyn was more faithful than anyone whom I ever knew to his old friends and always welcomed them gladly to the end of his life, but Alastair Graham, who was the closest of all his old friends, passed completely out of his life.

It will be seen from these anecdotes that there was a degree of truth in the accusation of homosexual affections against Evelyn, but the story must be seen in proportion. The Victorian habit was to speak of homosexual sins as the unmentionable sins. All pre-marital sex was evil, and to protect the boys at public schools from possibility of contamination they were never allowed under any circumstances to catch sight of a woman. Even the masters in those days were generally not married. The inevitable consequence of imposing such a regimen upon them in these delicate years was almost to force them into sentimental homosexual friendships. The policy of the authorities was to turn a blind eye on such friendships, so long as they did not lead to any overt physical act. When such an act was committed and when it came to light, horror was unbridled and the punishment of expulsion instant and unrelenting. George Lyttelton used to tell the story of a boy at Eton who was caught in such an offence. Doctor Warre's method of dealing with it was to summon the boy's father down to Eton and then, in front of the culprit, tell his parent of the enormous wickedness of which he had been guilty. The father said, 'Doctor Warre, Doctor Warre, I'd sooner that he was lying dead at my feet.' The boy was then duly expelled and handed over to his father and the pair were left to travel home together. It can hardly have been a very pleasant journey.

Much the same system continued up till the war and after it. It sometimes failed but more often had the effect of persuading the boys that, though homosexual friendships were perhaps innocent and inevitable, the act was nevertheless a heinous sin.

On the other hand the age was still an age of reticence, and, though such friendships might be indulged and freely discussed among the boys, a common embarrassment prevented any easy discussion of them between boys and masters or between masters and boys. Alec Waugh in his *The Loom of Youth* had discussed the prevalence of homosexual vice at Sherborne with a frankness which was at that time considered extremely shocking, but he had written in that book that, though such acts under the restriction of single-sex schools were almost inevitable and not particularly harmful, it was a great advantage of them that very few public school boys preserved such tastes into after life. Lancing, in Evelyn's day was, because of its Woodard High Church connection or for some other reason, apparently less permissive than Sherborne in the days of Alec, and Evelyn throughout his schooldays had no very deep affection for small boys. On revisiting the school as an old boy he was astonished at the obsessive prevalence of talk about such matters among the masters, but he had no suspicion of such prevalence during his own schooldays. He emerged from his schooldays virginal and expressing the opinion that sexual indulgence was 'unworthy of a man'. He allowed his tastes at Oxford to develop in a homosexual direction to the extent that we have indicated, because that was the general habit of Oxford at that day. The women had only recently been allowed degrees at Oxford. Their companionship with the male undergraduates was controlled by very strict rules. The males had for the most part no great wish for feminine company and did not admit them into their societies. The soldiers who had come back from the war and gone up to the University immediately after it were naturally more familiar with female company, but any attempts by them to introduce it into general University life was not much welcomed by the undergraduates who came up straight from school, and by the time that Evelyn reached Oxford in 1922 the warriors had almost entirely gone down and the traditional habits of Oxford life were able to reassert themselves. They did so with Evelyn as with others. Whether habits were different in the years after the war from what they had been before, who shall say? Pre-war reticence makes it impossible to form a judgment. Every age has its fashions in talk about unnatural habits. A hundred and fifty years ago everyone talked about incest. Today everyone talks about homosexuality, but my guess is that it is in fact less common than it was immediately before the 1914 war. The world and Oxford of the 1920's were in an intermediate stage. The undergraduate—at any rate those of the set which I am discussing—had few inhibitions about their exploits and confessed their amours to one another. But they did not publish them to their tutors or to the world. Evelyn was of that set. But in the long run he was, as were most of the others, a very complete example of Alec Waugh's saying. He was in no sort of way a confirmed and continuing homosexual, and, almost immediately after he went down, found his companionship among women and continued thus for the rest of his life.

Even in his undergraduate days he was not very incontinent in his conduct. 'My affections are much more romantic than carnal,' he once said to me at that time, and it was, I think, true. Later in life he was not indeed wholly chaste. 'I had never been in the least chaste until I met Laura,' he once said to me towards the end of his life. He went through a period of intense depression when the ecclesiastical law's delays held up interminably the granting of the annulment of his first marriage. He brought accusations of mendacity against some of the clergy with whom he had dealings and was for a time rather violently anti-clerical. He was then living at Mells and one day said to me, 'Do you think that Katharine [Mrs Asquith] would mind very much if I married outside the Church?' I said that I thought that she would. 'I suppose so,' he said, and I do not think that he ever seriously thought of doing such a thing, though ready at that time to maintain that 'one had to commit some sins'. 'Snip and be damned,' was his advice to a pious Catholic lady, who was told that she could not easily have another baby. Even at the end of his life during his years of happy marriage when his own sexual conduct was beyond reproach but when in general he was very free with his comments on other people's shortcomings he was never very censorious of those who had been guilty merely of fornication. On this shortcoming his comments were always restrained.

On the other hand he once in these later years told me how a distinguished Conservative Member of Parliament had asked him to sleep with his—the politician's—wife. He was much shocked and curtly refused. His activities were such on the whole as he ascribed to Gilbert Pinfold. He did not casually cohabit with his friends or with those whom he respected, but on occasion found in his bachelor state a purely physical and professional relief for a need which he felt. The commentator on the *Diaries* in the *Observer* raises a certain mystery about his expulsion from the second school at which he taught at Aston Clinton, but though he told his mother that he was dismissed for drunkenness, the fact, as he confessed to me, was that he was dismissed for trying to seduce the matron. But as for homosexuality, in all the years after Oxford he not only eschewed it but, as was his way, turned to a very violent condemnation of it—'a habit I happen very particularly to dislike,' he said of it one day in his club to a fellow member who had made against him such an accusation. I reported to him one day that a very highly respected ecclesiastic had said to me—as at that time many such were saying—that the laws against homosexual activities should be repealed. Evelyn refused to believe me. 'You must have misunderstood what he said,' he commented. Wilfrid Meynell once quoted to me the saying of a friend of his who had said, 'I consider the company of any woman preferable to that of any man.' I thought this an exaggeration and condemned it as such in repeating it to Evelyn. He would not agree. 'I should think that that was true,' he said.

It was our custom—doubtless a silly and immature custom—to indulge in meaninglessly crude language about people's sexual habits without attaching to it any serious significance. For instance if one person ever spoke to another we described it as 'lying with him'. This sometimes got us into trouble with those who did not understand our habits. Edmund Gosse, for instance, greatly and not unreasonably objected to the suggestion that he 'lay' with some lady with whom he had but the most casual of acquaintances and wrote to Arthur Waugh to say that he would be very glad to continue his friendship with him, who was his cousin, but that he on no account wished ever to see Evelyn again. In the *Diaries* I find recorded what Evelyn describes as an excellent story of mine. It seems that Lord Phillimore, a proper and strait-laced judge, had to try a case of buggery and he asked for advice from Lord Birkenhead who was then the Lord Chancellor. 'What ought I to give to a man who allows himself to be buggered?' he asked. 'Oh, thirty shillings, or two pounds—whatever you happen to have on you,' replied Birkenhead. I have no memory of having told such a story. My acquaintance with Lord Birkenhead was certainly not such that he would have confided it to me and I never met Lord Phillimore. So whence I can have derived it I cannot imagine, but Claud Cockburn the other day assured me that he remembered me telling it.

As for drunkenness it cannot be denied that Evelyn, like the rest of us, drank very heavily during those years at Oxford and that he continued doing so during the rest of his life. The exploits recorded in the *Diaries*, of some of which I was a witness and perhaps partaker and some not, are sufficient evidence of this habit, nor was this a habit which he at all changed with going down. The *Diaries* were not kept during his undergraduate days, but he resumed them immediately after going down. They had therefore more to tell about the exploits of his visits to Oxford during the year after he came down. I was then abroad on a debating trip, but my brother had just gone up to Worcester and he figures in an episode or two in those *Diaries*. We used to tell in the family of an escapade in which Evelyn, riding on a motor bicycle, picked up my brother from our home in Wells. He took him up into the Mendips to a pub in, I think, Chewton Mendip where they got liberally drunk. The problem was that of getting my brother home again. He was installed as a pillion-rider on the motor bicycle and they proceeded towards Wells. Unfortunately from time to time he fell off and had to be picked up again. When passing along the road we still mark the places of his collapse, in rather blasphemous fashion, as if they were the Stations of the Cross. 'Here is where Henry fell off for the third time,' we say, and so on. Eventually Evelyn got him to my father's house where he propped him up against the wall and left him.

In *Brideshead Revisited* it will be remembered that Ryder and Sebastian Flyte, when they were staying alone at Brideshead, gaily drank together in one another's company and agreed that they ought to get drunk every night. Gradually it dawned upon Ryder that there was a difference between his drinking and that of Sebastian. He drank because he enjoyed it, but with Sebastian drink was a disease and in the end he develops into a full dipsomaniac and as such finds refuge in a monastery in Tunis. Evelyn never allowed the characters of his novels to be mere portraits, and neither Hugh Lygon nor Alastair Graham, on whom Sebastian Flyte was based, though they were both heavy drinkers, were dipsomaniac, nor was Evelyn himself. Of course we all drank heavily. We drank beer rather than wine or whisky. We doubtless drank more because we knew nothing of drugs. I only remember one undergraduate of those days who, as far as I know, took drugs. Drink was much cheaper in those days than it is today. Scouts were more plentiful and it was still possible to give in one's room luncheon parties where various forms of cup flowed freely with the easy conversation and which often began at lunch and still went on until tea or even later. Evelyn, small in stature, would sit in a high chair in the Hypocrites Club with his large head lolling helplessly to one side in a very intoxicated condition. He had in all his potations a certain rule of self-respect. I remember sitting with him and Alastair Graham on the evening on which I had returned from my trip around the world. We had drunk well and he, who always drank very quickly, had drunk probably more than any of us. He begged us almost with tears that we would leave the room and not attend if he should be sick. For he could not bear the indignity of being observed to vomit.

He certainly never became an alcoholic. Yet one who observed him throughout his life must wonder whether he was as completely immune to the dangers of alcohol as he imagined both for Ryder and for himself. At one time during the war he was appointed PA to a certain Brigadier. Having received the appointment he at once proceeded that evening to get drunk in the Mess. The Brigadier said to him in rebuke that he could not have a PA who got 'foxed'—'an expression', said Evelyn, 'which was new to me.' Evelyn replied, 'Sir, you cannot expect me to abandon the habits of a lifetime for a purely temporary appointment.' Quite early in life he became strangely deficient in memory and was unable to recall events that had happened or people whom he had met quite recently. He very soon grew deaf and exploited his deficiency with an absurd ear-trumpet. He was unable to sleep and made reckless use of sleeping-pills on a scale far beyond what any doctor can have recommended. There was the strange *Ordeal of Gilbert Pinfold*. After he had returned from that visit to Ceylon I saw him one day in the church at Downside Abbey. 'How have you been keeping?' I asked. 'I've been mad,' he answered, 'What?' I said. 'Been mad!' he reiterated, his voice ringing out above the service that was in progress. 'I've been absolutely mad. Clean off my onion.'

In his last years he had adopted all the antics of an old man and addressed and welcomed his friends as such. 'It is very good of you to come,' he would say, leaning on his stick. My wife and I thought that this was something of an affectation and mocked him for it. Then one Sunday I received a telephone message from *The Times* to say that he had died that morning. His family had taken the telephone off the hook and *The Times* asked my advice how they could get in touch with them. I was commissioned by *The Times* to write his obituary notice, and did so. It is for a doctor to say whether any of his disabilities were the consequence of his habits of indulgence and whether he would have lived a little longer had he lived a little more carefully. He always, of course, in all his last years maintained that he had no wish to go on living.

An accusation that is very frequently made against him by his critics is that of absurd and exaggerated snobbery. It is impossible for one who reads his books or who follows the details of his life to deny that he did obviously seek out to an absurd extent the rich and the titled and preferred to cast his tales among them. Born and brought up in comparatively humble circumstances in Golders Green, he would walk to Hampstead to post his letters in order that they might bear a more aristocratic postmark. In later life when a headmaster suggested that his son would be well advised to read English Literature at Oxford, he replied, 'English Literature is no school for a gentleman.' The truly aristocratic found his pretensions slightly comic. My neighbour Conrad Russell of the Russell family who quite liked him said of him, 'I'm afraid not quite a gentleman—not quite—not quite.' Yet, in so far as we are concerned with his Oxford career, his companions in those days—those for instance who travelled with him on the Railway Club—were in no way aristocrats. Among all his friends the only peer was the present Earl of Wicklow, then Lord Clonmore, surely the least pompous and the least pretentious of all living peers. A few years later when they had both become Catholics, Evelyn in a spirit of comedy delated Billy Wicklow to the Fathers at Farm Street. 'I regret to report that last Saturday the Earl of Wicklow was seen assisting at an heretical wedding, drunk, devout and uninvited.' His only other friend of aristocratic origins was Hugh Lygon, the son of Lord Beauchamp, the former Liberal politician afterwards to live out of England under compulsion in circumstances not exactly parallel but similar to those of Lord Marchmain in *Brideshead Revisited*. Hugh, too, was hardly a pretentious aristocrat. The Duggans were indeed the stepsons of Lord Curzon, but can hardly be called aristocratic. Alfred Duggan was at that time a dipsomaniac Communist —later to become a pious, teetotal but very impoverished historical novelist. Indeed so far was Evelyn at that time from making aristocratic pretensions that the company of us who lunched on beer and cheese every day in his rooms at Hertford called ourselves Offal and contrasted ourselves with the not very blue-blooded athletes of the College whom we dubbed the Hertford Upper World. In his first novel, *Decline and Fall*, the county family undergraduates of Scone, baying for blood after their celebratory Bollinger dinner and callously bringing unmerited evil on poor middle-class Paul Pennyfeather, are by no means creatures held up to our admiration or likely to give an impression that Evelyn had an unduly high opinion of them. I myself had not the faintest claims to high birth. Yet neither at Oxford nor afterwards during his whole life did my

wife or I ever have a word of difference or unkindness from him, though
once he did complain a little when in an article, I said, very truly, that I
was not a gentleman. He very rightly held my wife in especially high
regard. For all his strangely reactionary opinions he never in any way
quarrelled with the left-wing friends whom he had acquired—Tom
Driberg, for instance, or Lord Longford.

As for the *saeva indignatio* which caused him to turn and rend without
mercy those who had incurred his displeasure or contempt? There can
be no question that in later life when he came to live almost a recluse's
life he justly incurred this charge. One day in the 1930's when we were
travelling in Greece, I noticed that every day he put himself to considerable trouble to obtain an English newspaper. I asked him why he did
this, as he was not much interested in current political affairs. 'Oh,' he
said, 'just to see if there is any good news which I might otherwise have
missed—such as, for instance, the death of Mrs Heygate.' (Mrs Heygate
was of course by then the name of his divorced wife, Evelyn Gardner.)
But this was not so complete an expression of absolute malice as it might
appear. When he became a Catholic he thought that he was condemning
himself to a permanent renunciation of marriage. Even later when he
learnt of the possibilities of an annulment the law's delays before he got
his decree were so intolerable as to drive him nearly to frenzy and it was
not wholly unnatural if he should have welcomed an act of God which
would have rescued him from those processes. Cyril Connolly, who had
indeed some reason to resent his bitter attacks and expressions of contempt, spoke of his 'bloated, puffed-up face . . . with the beady eyes red
with wine and anger, his cigar jabbing as he went into the attack'. He
refused in those days to answer the telephone. I remember one day a
manservant coming in to say, 'Mr Randolph Churchill would like to
speak to you on the telephone, sir.' 'Tell him to write,' said Evelyn. But
in his undergraduate days he was far from a cantankerous man. He had
indeed his enemies whom he attacked—sometimes with reason and
sometimes without reason—but in general he thought of himself as a
happy man and his days as happy days. He enjoyed company and parties
and in *A Little Learning* quotes of his Oxford days Belloc's lines:

> For noone, in our long decline,
>   So dusty, spiteful and divided,
> Had quite such pleasant friends as mine,
>   Or loved them half as much as I did.

He was much befriended and he was also much befriending. It was only a year later—after his immediate mishaps leading to his attempted suicide on the coast of Denbighshire—that he developed his habit of bitter complaint against the emptiness of life and even, for a time, I fear, against his own parents. There was an interval of five years between him and his brother Alec and at that time he accepted the idea—whether with any basis or not I cannot say—that he was an unwanted child. As a matter of fact, as between him and his admirable father he was much more sinning than sinned against. Unpardonable things were all too often on his lips in this period as he afterwards most fully recognised.

It was of course our habit, as indeed it was a pretty general habit of undergraduates, to speak with a certain genial contempt of Dons. They had not yet developed, as they have in our days, the habit of spending their time in rushing up to London to dabble on the Stock Exchange or to talk on television, to the neglect in some cases of their own pupils. Practically none of them had motor cars. They were doubtless learned in their subjects, perhaps more learned than their successors of today— but we were not greatly interested in their subjects. To us they were 'remote and ineffectual' Dons—not to be hated, not even to be despised, but not an important part of Oxford life, not much interfering with our lives but to be gently mocked. Only two of them, I fancy, fell under Evelyn's reprobation. Sligger Urquhart was the Dean of Balliol. His paths and those of Evelyn did not naturally cross, but he had asked Evelyn to lunch in the days of his companionship with Richard Pares and offered him barley water to drink—an error not easily to be forgiven. In his later terms Evelyn masterminded a genial but offensive campaign against him. He was guyed in Evelyn's comic film about the conversion of England to Rome. Sligger had, according to a report that reached us—I expect correctly—gone to Cambridge to deliver a lecture, but, arrived there, had been unable to deliver it because of an attack of hiccups. For some reason this intensely amused Evelyn and he caused us to parade around Balliol Quad, singing:

> Gawd help Urquharts on a night like this.
> Oop goes the Urquhart.

His far more serious quarrel was with Cruttwell, his tutor at Hertford and afterwards Principal of the College. It will be remembered that in *A Little Learning* he devotes a number of paragraphs to a somewhat unpleasantly detailed account of Cruttwell's physical deficiency which caused him to dribble at the mouth. A buffoon character to whom he gives the name of Cruttwell appears in novel after novel, right up to

*Scoop* which appeared just before the Second World War. Cruttwell was
so unfortunate as in one of his lectures to let drop the incidental observa-
tion—I do not know in what context—'Of course a dog cannot have
rights.' For this a quite absurd saga of Cruttwell's intimate and improper
relations with dogs was invented. We congregated outside his rooms and
barked in imitation of dogs. Evelyn invented a ridiculous rhyme:

> Cruttwell dog, Cruttwell dog, where have you been?
> I've been to Hertford to lie with the Dean.
> Cruttwell dog, Cruttwell dog, what did you there?
> I bit off his penis and pubic hair.

He would shout this across Hertford Quad.

Now Cruttwell had his acerbic defects, but it was not at all easy to
see what grave harm he could ever have done to Evelyn that could have
justified this so great hate. Doubtless he had on occasion let drop some
words of rebuke at his neglect of his work, but, since Evelyn was a
scholar of the College and he was his tutor, he could hardly be blamed
for that. Evelyn once confessed to me, 'Really, Cruttwell is rather better
than most of the Dons. But one must have someone to persecute.' Yet
he was content not merely to mock him and quarrel with him at the
time, but to continue the quarrel in an absurd way long after their paths
had ceased to cross—long after, indeed, Cruttwell had died—I believe in
a lunatic asylum. To the offensive passages in *A Little Learning*—in
general so kindly and urbane a book—I have already referred. They were
written long after Cruttwell's and shortly before Evelyn's own death. It
is a strange story, reminding one of Bismarck in his old age recreating
himself by indulging in orgies of hate against his old schoolmaster of
seventy years before. When he had to fill in a form, for some work of
reference, of books which he had composed Evelyn amused himself by
entering *The Mind and Face of Cruttwell, Cruttwell from Within* and
similar absurdities. When in 1935 Cruttwell stood as Conservative
candidate for the University and owing to the complications of propor-
tional representation received so few of the first preference votes that he
forfeited his deposit, Evelyn when he heard the news happened to be in
Abyssinia. He hired a fleet of camels loaded with cleft clothes-pegs to
carry express messages, to be hastily telegraphed back in expression of
his joy.

It was his habit to adopt comic phrases descriptive of his acquaintances. These descriptions were sometimes wounding and insensitive.
There were, for instance, two fellow undergraduates who had been

companions and his friends at Lancing. Neither had ever done him any harm, nor did he greatly dislike them. One was Hugh Molson, now Lord Molson, a distinguished and successful Conversative politician. Before he came to Lancing he had been a cadet in the Navy at Dartmouth and there, according to Evelyn's often repeated tale, he had once been so misguided as to call the drill-sergeant 'a blasted liar'. For that he was condemned to a special form of grave punishment, which was considered to involve great ignominy and which could be inflicted only with the express leave of the First Lord of the Admiralty. Such permission was applied for and, according to Evelyn, the reply was received, 'You may beat Cadet Molson—Winston Churchill.' How much of this anecdote was true I cannot say. It cannot in the nature of things have been wholly true, as Winston Churchill was not First Lord of the Admiralty in those years after the 1918 armistice when alone the incident can possibly have occurred.

As I have said, it was our custom to forgather in Evelyn's room at lunchtime for what we knew as Offal—a meal of beer and cheese. One day going down the Broad to this assignation I met Hugh Molson outside Blackwell's shop and, since the membership of Offal was fluctuating and indeterminate, I explained what it was and invited him to join us. He drew himself up to his not very significant height and said, 'I usually prefer to have a hot lunch.' The reply seemed to us pompous and comic and indeed until this day the nickname of 'Hot Lunch Molson' has in a measure remained with him. In *A Little Learning* Evelyn ascribed the invention of the name to a very remarkable eccentric friend of his, Terence Greenidge, who had the habit of collecting all the stray pieces of paper which he found in the street, putting them in his pocket and at a convenient moment depositing them on Evelyn's floor. I do not wish to deprive Terence of any appropriate honour for he was a friend of mine, but I fancy that it was I who was responsible for the invention of 'Hot Lunch'. Terence arranged an absurd cinema film. It had never before occurred to me that cinema acting was an activity that any human being could take seriously, but in that film I found myself cast as a very villainous President of the Union.

Another friend of Evelyn was Roger Fulford, who was at Worcester. He was then and has remained ever since a man of some distinction and wholly respectable. He was President of the Union and has since won success as a Liberal politician and a student of the antics of monarchy. For no reason at all that I can imagine Evelyn saw fit to designate him 'Sub-Man Fulford'. The designation can hardly have been thought of as kindly.

It will be remembered that in *Decline and Fall* two of the absurd characters at Llanabba School are called Philbrick and Prendergast. Prendergast was a fellow master of Paul Pennyfather, Philbrick the school butler. Both end up in prison, Philbrick as prisoner, Prendergast as the prison chaplain, and Prendergast is murdered. There were two undergraduates of those names at Balliol in Evelyn's time. Prendergast, happily still with us, was a wholly virtuous and inoffensive aesthete who had never, I fancy, done any harm to Evelyn except once, it seems, make some remark to Peter Quennell about the undesirable bohemian company which he entertained when he found Evelyn in Quennell's room. Philbrick was an able but indiscreet scientist who had confessed, or was alleged to have confessed, that at school he had derived pleasure from the beating of smaller boys. Evelyn had got hold of this story and very mischievously spread all round the University the tale that Philbrick was an unbridled sadist. It happened shortly afterwards that in a film shown at one of the Oxford cinemas about African life there was a shot of some poor African being flogged. When this was shown on the screen there were cries from every quarter of the cinema of 'Philbrick, Philbrick'. The episode must have caused him very considerable embarrassment. On the night on which I was elected President of the Union I gave a party in my rooms in Balliol. Evelyn was present at it. The next evening I found in the passage that connects the Garden Quad with the New Quad at Balliol a large parti-coloured South Sea Island walking-stick which it was Evelyn's habit to carry around with him. I retrieved it and took it round to Hertford to give it back. He then told me that Philbrick and Basil Murray had waylaid him on the way back from my room and beaten him up. 'We did not attack you in Chris's room', they said, 'because it would have been embarrassing for him, but we have had as much of you as we can stand and now, by God, you're going to get it.'

Philbrick certainly had cause for complaint against Evelyn. I do not know what grievance Basil Murray had, but Evelyn had been in truculent mood that night and I expect that he had given Basil some cause for complaint. As with Evelyn himself, there was no necessity for the cause to be adequate if Basil Murray was in the mood to pick a quarrel. I remember once going with him to Chewton Mendip races, where he picked a quarrel with the men who were exploiting the three-card trick and was pursued by them back to the pub with cries of 'Look at 'im with his Osker Wild stockings on.'—which was in the company of such repartees comparatively accurate. Evelyn in *A Little Learning* speaks of him as 'a satanic character,' says that he did not like him, as he may well not have done, but confesses that among the company of dreary and undistinguished undergraduates he had a certain 'style'. I knew him a great deal better than Evelyn did. I would not pretend that it was possible to consider him as a fit candidate for canonisation. Still I think 'satanic' is an exaggeration. He was the son of Gilbert Murray, the famous Greek scholar and Liberal politician and champion of the League of Nations, and of Lady Mary Murray, of the Carlisle family.

The Carlisle family—the Howards—had in their blood an unfortunate trait of alcoholism. It was the belief of old Lady Carlisle that no Howard could touch alcohol without becoming a dipsomaniac—in which she may have been right—and also that this disability was shared by all mankind—in which she was certainly wrong. She therefore took all the abundant store of wine at Castle Howard and poured it into the surrounding moat—an act which brought down upon her considerable adverse criticism, particularly from F. E. Smith who thought that the liquor might well have been put to better purpose. Her daughter, Lady Mary, inherited her mother's prohibitionist principles and she in her turn infected with them her husband, Gilbert. They were also vegetarians and of the Left in politics. 'From our point of view, which is the Socialist,' explained Lady Mary, 'we must put things in their proper priorities. First there is the drink. As long as the poor are allowed to fuddle up their brains with this disgusting poison we cannot expect them to think sensibly about anything else. Then when we have got rid of the drink we can turn our minds to redistributing their property.' She was of that particular type of aristocratic politician who is enormously conscious of the great gap between herself and the working classes and thought of the latter as pawns whom it was her duty to rearrange for their undoubted good—just the type which Orwell most delighted to expose and mock.

Evelyn comments on it as unexpected that Basil should have been the product of such a stock. I do not think it so surprising. Rabid and irrational puritanism often has the effect of turning those upon whom it is imposed into exaggerated libertinism and, as a matter of fact, it was not only Basil among the Murray children who reacted against the very strict ways in which they had been brought up. When he came up as an undergraduate Basil soon broke with the parental rule of absolutely strict teetotalism. But, in spite of the Howard blood, he did not become a complete drunkard. On the other hand his life was generally dissipated. He was not very exact in money matters nor very strict in sexual conduct. He was factious and his life full of quarrels, very many of them unnecessary and about very little. Though a scholar of New College, he neglected

his books and did very badly in his schools. In this he was not indeed
very different from the rest of us, but, while to others lack of success in
schools was accepted by parents with a reasonable sense of proportion,
to Gilbert Murray to get only a Third in Mods was a blow similar to that
which a very serious clergyman or a pious Catholic might have suffered
had his son lost his faith. After a turbulent life and a broken marriage
Basil became involved in the Spanish Civil War and died in Spain.

'Why does everyone except me find it so easy to be nice?' Evelyn
makes Gilbert Pinfold ask. Certainly there were forces of evil at work
within him in conflict with the forces of good. Hyde was at constant
warfare with Jekyll, and, like Péguy's *pêcheur*, he came to the search of
God largely through his experience of the horror of a life divorced from
His company. Hilaire Belloc said of him at their first meeting, 'He is
possessed.' L. A. G. Strong, a poet, novelist and critic, who was at that
time a master at Summer Fields School, was an Irishman, a devotee of
J. M. Synge and a little tinged with W. B. Yeats's Celtic whimsy-
whamsy. He came to luncheon with me one day to meet Evelyn and
confided in me that he had throughout the meal seen evil, elemental
spirits dancing behind Evelyn's chair. I thought it great rubbish. Yet
whatever the truth of his anecdotes about Philbrick, Evelyn was
certainly not justified in making a guy of him and his alleged habits, for
he himself, when later, after his exploits in North Wales, he went to teach
at Aston Clinton, was quite frank and unashamed about the pleasure
that he derived from caning the boys there. He was quite popular at that
school from the engaging anecdotes which he used to tell the boys and
maintained—whether truly or not—that, provided that he afterwards
gave him a tie or a few sweets as recompense, the victim enjoyed being
caned. In any event Evelyn made no pretence that the operation was
meant seriously as a punishment for misdemeanour. It was a frank
pleasure.

He of course believed in the luxuries and indulgences, but also in the
physical rigours of life. As he showed in *Mr Loveday's Little Outing*
and *Love among the Ruins* or in the prison chapters of *Decline and Fall*,
any suggestion for modifying the penal code he dismissed with ridicule.
Punishment should be stern and without exception. He was full of contempt when, as a Member of Parliament, I supported the motion for the
abolition of capital punishment. He argued that murderers might well
be on many occasions not very wicked people, but on the other hand
nothing could be less charitable, to the unbalanced man afflicted with a
propensity to crime, than to allow him to go on living with the risk that

he could likely enough commit more crimes and sins. How much more religious and charitable to give him warning when he was to be killed and full opportunity to prepare his soul and then to lead him up to the scaffold in a state of grace! I argued with him that, if it was so great a good fortune for murderers to be hanged after due notice, would it not be a great kindness to all of us that we should be hanged even though we had not gone through the preliminary formality of murdering anyone?

I do not remember that he ever particularly developed any of these theories in his Oxford days, but I do remember at the Oxford Union, when the general habit was to air liberal opinions and to condemn the Treaty of Versailles and the like, that he went down and made a speech in favour of national hatred, as the one emotion that had given strength and value to the national character during the war and as a main cause of our artistic achievements through the ages. He never took any great interest then or at any other time in the battles of party politics. He stood for the Secretaryship of the Union but polled very badly. The only electoral activity in which he ever, I think, took part was of a not very creditable nature. In the elections of 1922 and 1923 Churchill had been defeated. He then stood as a candidate at a by-election for the Abbey division of Westminster. Evelyn and I agreed to canvass for him. We called at his committee rooms for election cards and obediently canvassed a voter or two without, as far as we could see, the smallest success. Luncheon time found us drinking at the Café Royal, and, having wearied of our task, we decided that we would do no more and returned our cards to the committee rooms. We agreed together that, if Churchill should be defeated by less than 60, we would have a feeling of guilt. The next day the result was declared and Churchill was defeated by 43.

Evelyn frankly enjoyed violence and conflict. Later in the 1930's he had no sort of sympathy with Sir Oswald Mosley and his Fascists and still less of course with Moseley's Communist opponents, but when I once said that I hoped that conflicts between them would not come to civil war and bloodshed he took issue with me. 'You must want bloodshed,' he said. 'Life is intolerable without it.'

In later life he refused to vote and in an often quoted *mot* said, 'I would consider it an impertinence to advise my sovereign on whom she should select for the government of her country.' This was too frequently quoted as an expression of serious opinion. Of course, it was obviously only said in order to rile his critics. Yet it did express his serious expression of 'God's scorn for all men governing', and also for all men governed.

It would be of course absurd to pretend that the story of Evelyn Waugh was the story of all Oxford in the 1920's. Our clique was a very small clique and our existence quite unknown to the great majority of undergraduates. It never occurred to us that he would turn out to be the best-known undergraduate of his generation. But so it has undoubtedly happened. The Union figures of that age have not proved to be politicians of the first importance. University scholars have not won world-wide reputations. University athletes have not been what they were before the war.

Evelyn did not at all share the passion of his father and his brother for cricket, and sport played no part in his life save under considerable protest. 'Very well, we will go to the Parks and see the black men batting in,' he said in resignation and protest to my suggestion that we go to see a little of the match between the University and the West Indies. In general we did not at all foresee the eminence that was to await him. We were conscious enough of his defects which seemed as evident as those of the rest of us. He had no music. At that date his architectural interests were limited. He knew nothing of foreign countries, none of which he had at that time visited, nor of foreign literature.

We doubtless thought that, like the rest of us, he would in some way make a living in the future. For it was still an age when boys who had been to public schools took it for granted that the world, in some way owed, or at least would give them a living. But we did not greatly bother about such problems whether for him or for any of the rest of us. Whatever secret ambitions any of us may have nourished we thought it the height of vulgarity to confess to them and would have imagined that he was the same. We were intent, as he was intent, on having a happy time.

Oxford was to us as it was to John Betjeman,

> That sweet hot-house world of bells
> And crumbling walls of golden-brown
> And dotty peers and incense-smells
> And dinners at the George and hock
> And Wytham Woods and Godstow Lock.

(Only the George is now no more.)

He wrote, as I remember, a story or two for the *Isis* or the *Cherwell* and reported the Union debates for those papers. 'It was a great pleasure to meet again the harsh voice and ungainly gestures of Mr Christopher Hollis,' he reported of a speech of mine. But we did not think of him seriously as a writer. We saw the book-cuts, book-headings and name-plates that he did and admitted their quality. We thought that such a minor art was his *métier*, a minor William Morris, said Harold Acton. He at one time suggested that he would do the book-cuts and I should write the verses for a book on Oxford eccentricities in which we would collaborate. Most unhappily I was too lazy to do my part. As it turned out it would have been an important entry into literary life to have entered it under Waugh's collaboration. As it was we none of us took his art very seriously and I was surprised when one day he said to me, 'I would give up my drink if I really thought that it interfered with my art.' I expressed my surprise. 'Yes, I would,' he insisted, 'because I think that my art is by far the nobler of the two.' I was yet more surprised at his choice of the word 'noble' for these little woodcuts.

# Harold Acton

Like Balaclava, the lava came down from the roof.
*Beelzebub at the Hotel*—Edith Sitwell

Of the other four subjects of essays in this volume, I do not suppose that
Harold Acton ever heard of Robertson-Glasgow or Robertson-Glasgow
of him. I expect that he must have heard the name of Hore-Belisha but
know of no record that they ever met, nor, if they did, would they have
had much in common. Harold Acton never played any part in Oxford's
Union or political life. He only once spoke at the Union, against the
motion, 'That this House would have preferred to have lived in the days
of its grandparents.' He championed the modern generation. The artist
is of his nature always trying to find the exact expression of his thought
—the *mot juste*—irrespective of its effect. The politician is always concerned with reservations and ambiguities that will safeguard him against
accusations of having broken the party line or prevent him from getting
into trouble with his constituents. There is therefore a natural antagon-
ism between the two. The only practising politician whom I ever heard
of Harold Acton having met was Brendan Bracken and he did not at all
like him. 'He used to blow in and out of Lord Faringdon's little house,
while I was staying there in the mid-twenties,' records Harold. 'I remember he had much in common with Peter Rodd of whom he seemed a pal,
at least to bandy words and arguments with, chiefly on political subjects
which didn't interest me. He was then a tough, rattling young dynamo
on the surface—Australian, I suspected, with a swaggering combative
approach. Apparently that sort of blustering, egocentric type appealed
to Winston Churchill, though I'm sure Churchill was too devoted to
his wife to beget bastards even in Bacchic mood. The impression that
remains is of a gross philistine with a button-holing hail-fellow-well-met
manner who might have been effective as a tough guy on the stage or

screen, throwing his weight about lustily. Personally he was antipathetic
to me.' Ready enough at times to hint at the quite baseless claim that
he was Churchill's illegitimate son, Bracken returned from a visit to
Roosevelt, so filled with such extravagant eulogy of the American
President that Randolph Churchill said, 'Brendan, are you going to say
that he was your father, too?' Harold Acton detested the fixing of deals
in which Bracken delighted. His judgment of Bracken may not have
been very accurate nor would he have been well acquainted with the
differences between Bracken and Belisha but he would doubtless have
thought, rightly or wrongly, of them as very much the same sort of
people and disliked the one as much as the other. On the other hand of
the two other subjects of essays—Maurice Bowra and Evelyn Waugh—
he knew Bowra fairly well and Evelyn, to whom he was best man at his
first wedding and who dedicated to him his first novel, *Decline and Fall,*
very intimately.

Harold Acton was slightly younger than Evelyn or the rest of us, hard
as it was to believe it. He was born in 1904, Evelyn in 1903. He only
came to Oxford, to Christ Church in October 1923, Evelyn in January,
1922. Yet he almost at once imposed himself on Oxford society and we
all of us—even as dominating a character as Evelyn—admitted his predominance. He proclaimed his poems and those of T. S. Eliot from his
rooms in Christ Church Meadow Quad through a megaphone to the
passing company, and his eccentricity was accepted. At his first arrival
there was hostility to him as a 'bloody aesthete'. And of his fellow undergraduates at the House, Sir Alec Douglas-Home (then Lord Dunglass)
—the perfect schoolboy, member of the Eleven and President of Pop
at Eton—particularly disapproved of such prominence being accorded
to one who had won no athletic colours and who did not even take games
seriously. However, the athletes of Vincent's Club with that excellent
good nature of the English upper class in all but their most bloody
moods were soon won over by his friendliness and cordiality, asked him
to dinner and found the meal a very great success, much enjoyed by both
hosts and guest.

The reason why Harold Acton was able to establish this general
predominance over us was this. He had a vivid personality which would
doubtless in any event have won him public notice, but his special distinction was his foreign experience. A consequence of the war was that the
ordinary undergraduate of those years immediately after the armistice
had of course no experience of foreign travel. Evelyn Waugh, for
instance, at that time had never been out of England, nor had Harold

Acton's fellow aesthete, Brian Howard. My own foreign travel was confined to a single bicycle trip through Brittany. Even older men like Bowra who had fought in the war knew of Western Europe only through the experience in the trenches. Maurice of the older generation had been brought up in China from school in England and had travelled through Russia on his way there but at that date he knew nothing of Western Europe as a place of culture. He had not as yet visited any of its picture galleries. We had ambitions of travel—but no more. Evelyn and I had a plan for going to Cefalù to rescue someone—I forget exactly who—from Aleister Crowley, but nothing came of it and we never made the trip.

Now in contrast to all this Harold Acton, legally indeed an Englishman, was the son of an *inglese italianato*, a lover and collector of objects of art, who lived just outside Florence. He alone of his family had preserved British nationality. Almost all Harold's other relatives were Americans and he himself had been brought up in Florence. In his early years he had only left Italy to go to America. He had never been to England until just before the war when he went for a short time to a preparatory school at Wokingham. Thence he went to Eton, entirely unfamiliar with English ways and English games and the attitude towards English games. He went in great dread, expecting to be enormously unhappy. In fact it did not turn out nearly as badly as he had feared. Nevertheless all the important cultural experiences of his life were the experiences that he had acquired outside England. Of these almost all the rest of us were grossly ignorant. Cyril Connolly indeed, even at that age, knew a considerable amount about French poetry. Kenneth Clark had early acquired his love for Italian painting and his love had been judiciously, if erratically, fostered at Winchester by Monty Rendall, the Headmaster. Anthony Powell, I expect, had already taken himself to Proust. The rest of us were ignorant. Evelyn in particular was ignorant. Neither then nor indeed at any other time did he know much or care much about French literature. He prided himself on his obstinate John Bullishness and ignored all foreign languages. He would argue that no one who knew more than one language could ever memorably express himself in any. He cited Mezzofanti, about whom I do not think that he knew anything but by hearsay, and Maurice Baring. The multi-linguist, he argued, when challenged to say something expressive and memorable, evaded the challenge to find the *mot juste* by taking refuge in the phrase from another language. He would most certainly have agreed with the liaison officer to the Free French in Anthony Powell's *The Soldier's Art* that speaking another language tolerably well seems so often to go with 'unsatisfactory habits'.

Now Harold Acton had been brought up in culturally cosmopolitan society. It is true that he was of course then still only a child and could hardly expect to join in the conversation of pundits like Bernard Berenson, whom he heard around him. But, as he himself said, he was born old and always delighted to listen to cultural talk even at an age when he was not yet able to any important extent to join in it. He brought into Oxford an air of cosmopolitan culture which it sadly lacked. We heard from him all sorts of names of which we should have heard but of which we were in fact sadly ignorant. I remember well one evening at the George hearing from him of Jean Cocteau, with whose name up till then I was boorishly unacquainted. This cosmopolitan knowledge gave him a great but not an unmixed advantage over the rest of us. He was enormously our superior in his knowledge of Continental literature, pictures or architecture. On the other hand he knew little of English literature. I remember well a dinner one evening at the Golden Cross, when Harold referred to Dickens with great contempt as 'a writer whom my nurse used to make me read'. He obviously knew little about him. Evelyn, who had been brought up by his excellent father, a man of letters, to tread well the central paths of English and especially Victorian literature, even if he knew little of what he called 'bloody abroad', knew and admired his Dickens well and took Harold severely to task. For all his interest in ecclesiastical architecture I never came across any hint of Harold ever visiting any English cathedral.

If Harold had been a boring pedant doubtless we would have continued in our ignorance and preferred to remain uncultured, but he wore his culture with such an air of high spirits, kindliness and good humour, with so brave a dash that we all fell for him and even those who came to scoff were soon persuaded to remain, if not to pray, at least to laugh. With his tall, distinguished, vaguely Oriental looks, with the scarf carelessly twisted round his neck, most of us did not remember, and doubtless many did not know, that he was really younger than the rest of us. We accepted him without complaint as our leader and hardly recollected that he had been still a schoolboy when we were already undergraduates.

An exact contemporary of mine at Balliol, as he had also been at Eton, was a young man, short of stature, by the name of Peter Cardew. He was and is a very worthy citizen, who has subsequently risen to high prosperity in the world of tobacco. He was good enough at his books but he was not a boy who made any pretensions to playing a part of distinction

in the aesthetic world. Owing to the fact that I had been at school with
him and that then he was at the same College as I was, I was friendly with
him but he would not naturally have been at all known to the aesthetic
group that gathered around Harold Acton. However, he had not only
been at Eton with Harold but had also been at the same House and he
became a figure of great notoriety through Harold's confession that at
Eton he had been beaten—'tanned'—by him. 'One day', explained
Harold, in his carefully articulated Italian accent, interspersed as it was,
with a dash of American slang, 'he called me down to the library and put
me through an examination in the football house colours of the various
houses. Of course I did not know any of them. How could one know a
thing like that? So he said, "It is disgraceful. You must be tanned." I
had to bend over a chair and he hit me with a stick called a pop-cane.
Smack, smack, smack. I shifted round so that the blows might fall in a
different place. "Keep still," he shouted. "It's my religion. I'm turning
the other cheek," I said. He thought I was impertinent. Did it hurt? Oh,
it was agony at the time, as the blows fell, like being branded with
molten iron but one felt, oh such a frisson of excitement when it was all
over like—like well, you know like what!' Harold's friends used to stop
Peter Cardew and ask him, 'Is it true that you beat Harold Acton?' To
him the operation was merely a normal incident of public school life,
unmemorable and hardly remembered. 'I expect so. Why do you ask?'
but others looked with awe on the hand that had thus dared to break the
cane across the imperial bottom.

As I say, Harold Acton had gone to Eton, knowing nothing of the
ways of English schools or of the life there. Games—'footer', as Anthony
Blanche in *Brideshead Revisited*, the heroic aesthete who was to some
extent based on Harold, calls it—was of no interest to him. However,
the demands of an English public school were to him so bizarre that with
his excellent good nature he had no wish obstinately to rebel against its
fashions, provided only that he was allowed, while conforming to the
demands of others, at the same time to conform to the demands of his
own nature. It is the virtue of Eton that it is so large a school that there
is room in it for the nonconformist. Public schools are commonly accused
of too great insistence on conformity to the type. The accusation may
be true of some schools—particularly of those which are less assured and
are struggling for recognition. But Harold knew nothing of any school
in England except Eton. It could not be denied that even at Eton the
intolerant athletic philistine, despising the arts or the intellect, was sometimes found and Harold, with his gay and unsuspecting good nature,

perhaps underrated the criticism with which he was discussed in certain circles. But its arrogance and its large numbers made Eton perhaps more ready to extend tolerance than other schools. It is so much more important to be an Etonian than not to be an Etonian that eccentricity—even artistic proclivities or foreign habits—can be forgiven, and Harold left Eton with quite kindly feelings and with a conviction that, even if he had not been educated there, he had at any rate been tolerated by the lordly Olympians who found him quite amusing. He never felt under any temptation to imitate the rather cheap flippancy of Osbert Sitwell, who entered as his education in *Who's Who*, 'During the holidays from Eton.'

His two housemasters, first Hugh de Havilland and then Archibald McNeill, a rigid Ulster militarist of small imagination, were not men from whom he derived much assistance, but he fell under the spell of the most admirable drawing master, Mr Evans. I myself was no sort of draughtsman and therefore in my day never had any connection with Mr Evans, but a great friend of mine, David Keswick, the brother incidentally of John Keswick with whom Harold was to form an intimate friendship in China, had considerable artistic capacities and Mr Evans befriended him. He helped him to write a paper about Degas for the Essay Society, from which I for the first time, I fancy, learnt of the existence of that artist. But David, for all his artistic and aesthetic pretensions, never had any mind to make a profession out of such a thing. His career was that of the normally successful schoolboy. He got his House colours, was elected to Pop on the same day as I was, and afterwards, after a successful career at Trinity College, Cambridge, became a wealthy banker with Samuel, Montagu. He now farms in Dumfriesshire.

Harold's career a few years later was different. He was defiantly an aesthete. His ambition was to be a poet. He received encouragement from Mr Evans and under this encouragement formed the Eton Society of Arts. He found kindred souls with whom he could co-operate—Oliver Messel, Brian Howard, a year or two afterwards to challenge his title to be the leading aesthete of the Oxford of his day—Robert Byron, then the great devotee of Ruskin—Alan Clutton-Brock, the son of the critic with whom Hilaire Belloc had had his dispute about the authorship of the Gospels—Cyril Connolly, Anthony Powell, then mainly interested in book illustrations and Lovat Fraser, Henry Yorke, later to become the successful novelist under the *nom de plume* of Henry Green. Orwell, still owning to his real name of Eric Blair, was then at Eton. He was a little older than they, and, though Harold Acton just knew him, he was by no means of their set, with which indeed he would not have had much sympathy. I was a year or two older and had left Eton a few years before, but once on a visit to the school I attended one of their exhibitions at which Alan Clutton-Brock showed some mural decorations painted in oils on a surface of handmade marble paper.

Harold Acton's most constant companion in those days was Brian Howard with whom he enjoyed a running intermission of friendship and enmity—at one time going about with him in constant companionship, at another in such hostility that he knocked him through a plate glass window. My own relations with Brian Howard were never good—entirely through my own fault. He had a curious uppish insolence. I remember how at the age of, I suppose, sixteen, he gave the riposte direct to the very distinguished septuagenarian ex-disciple of Ruskin, Mr Luxmoore, saying to him, 'Personally I have always found Canaletto a very vulgar painter.' He and I were neither of us gentlemen—which was comparatively rare among Etonians of that day—but he had an ambition to pass himself off as such which I in no way shared. He and Harold Acton produced together during their last half at Eton a literary magazine called *The Eton Candle*, which was sarcastically named by some the *Eton Scandal* but which attracted the favour of Edith Sitwell who thus for the first time came into Harold's life.

He then went up to Oxford to Christ Church, heralding his arrival there by publishing his first book of poems, *Aquarium*. At Christ Church in his rooms in Meadow Quad he from the first established himself as the dominant leader of the young aesthetes of the day. He introduced the habit of wearing broad trousers, which soon afterwards obtained general popularity under the title of 'Oxford bags', and with Robert Byron as an ally he inaugurated the fashion for the admiration for early Victorian habits. Some of his comments on Victorians were characteristically light-hearted.

> Who was the genuine Jack the Ripper?
> Was he a sailor? Was he a skipper?
> Was he a tailor? Was he a tinker?
> Was he a great Victorian thinker?

He visited Lady Ottoline Morrell at Garsington and gave great offence there by writing a poem commenting on her husband Philip Morrell's alleged embarrassment at the company in which he found himself,

> 'Their husbands do not share the fun.'

But Lady Ottoline was accustomed to being guyed by her guests and Harold's offence was small in comparison with that of D. H. Lawrence and Aldous Huxley. She was mercilessly guyed as Hermione Roddice in Lawrence's *Women in Love* and as Priscilla Wimbush in Huxley's *Crome Yellow*, and Logan Pearsall Smith persecuted her with anecdotes of unflagging hostility.

As with all that he did, Harold was half serious and half comic. He always had an admirable talent for signifying his own antics with a pleasant little friendly chuckle. He started a magazine called the *Oxford Broom* and became a frequenter of Oxford societies, always ready enough to respond to any invitation to read a paper to them. His ambitions at that time were, almost entirely, those of a poet and his campaign was to denounce the fashionable Georgian poets of John Squire's *London Mercury*—what he called the Squire-archy—devotees of beer and village cricket. Squire at that time used to come down to Oxford to inspect the rising young poets and prided himself on being their patron. Patrick Ryan wrote of him:

> I'm Jack
> From the shack
> Where the knack
> Of writing verse is known.

Squire was not perhaps taken quite as seriously by undergraduates as he took himself. In opposition to the Georgians, Harold did not declaim French or Italian poets, who would perhaps have been too incomprehensible and unfashionable for Oxford undergraduates, but gave us instead the Sitwells or T. S. Eliot and his 'Prufrock'. He introduced us to Rimbaud and Gerard Manley Hopkins.

One of his haunts was the notorious Hypocrites down beyond Christ Church, where the presiding spirits were Richard Hughes and Robert Graves. Robert Graves then lived up on Boars Hill, Richard Hughes was still an undergraduate at Oriel. Skelton was their laureate. It was a boozing house where shove-halfpenny and dart playing were the fashion, where much beer was drunk, Graham Pollard, a Communist and a book collector, the son of the distinguished historian, himself was to be found there—and Richard Pares, the friend of Evelyn Waugh—Mark Ogilvie Grant, a friend of Harold from his private school days—John Lloyd of Montgomery, commonly known as the Widow Lloyd—Keith Douglas and Peter Ruffer, Ruffer was a very fat melancholic man who took up slimming and eventually slimmed himself to death.

Intimate among Harold's friends of this description was the remarkable John Sutro, the best of friends and the most adept of all mimics, the nephew of the dramatist. He had a passion for railways and organised the Railway Club, by which he arranged with the Great Western authorities for its members, his friends, to take a journey one evening on a train which would be served with a special dinner. We travelled over the Penzance–Aberdeen express line from Oxford to Leicester, then debouched and walked the platform at Leicester for half an hour. We then boarded a returning train and travelled back to Oxford, refreshed *en route* by brandy and liqueurs.

Harold Acton also collaborated in those days with Robert Byron in organising a display of early Victorian domestic ornaments but for some unexplained reason it met with the disapproval of the authorities and was banned by the Proctors. Robert in his campaign against anti-Victorianism at this period had not yet developed his Byzantine interests and professed instead a vigorous traditional Protestantism. In this he was joined by Billy Clonmore, himself afterwards to become a most devoted Catholic convert but at that time a contented Anglo-Irish Protestant. He had been a great friend of Harold at Eton where he was slightly his senior, and had been the first to welcome him with hospitality when he came up to Oxford. They showed a film of the Crusaders at the Hypocrites and Byron and Clonmore attended it, greeting any passing repulse in battle of the Crusaders with loud cries of 'Down with the Roman Catholics'. This was an escapade with which Harold had no sympathy, and their joint project for organising a Queen Victoria ballet in which Byron would impersonate the Queen not being amused and Harold, hidden behind a false beard, would lurk in the background taking notes, as an impersonation of Lytton Strachey, equally failed to materialise.

Harold loved company and 'the noise and the dust of many men'. He had no love of solitude. He wrote:

> And Nietzsche did not know his loss,
>   When mealy-mannered, he declared,
> Alone, like a rhinoceros
>   I wander through a thankless world.

But the instructors at whose feet Harold at that time sat were the Sitwells —the two brothers and their sister—and after them, rather with tongue in cheek, Gertrude Stein. None of them, I think, was very well known at Oxford before Harold's introduction, and the general fashion was to think of them rather as figures of innocent fun than as serious writers.

Harold had first met Edith Sitwell at a party in London a few months before. He accepted her as his main champion in the battle against the Georgian poets. He and Evelyn shouted round the quad at night the lines from her *Beelzebub When Sir*:

> Like Balaclava, the lava came down from the
> Roof, and the sea's blue-wooden gendarmerie
> Took them in charge, while Beelzebub roared for his rum
> . . . None of them come!

He invited her down to address the Ordinary Society, a group at whose normal meetings poetical undergraduates sat round the room, reading one another's recent compositions. He had hired the room for an audience of seventy people and prepared for her sustenance a mammoth Swiss roll, decorated with pink and white sugar. I remember well the occasion. She delivered a violent attack on the critics of the day who had ventured to pour scorn on her or her brother Osbert. She dismissed D. H. Lawrence as 'the head of the Jaeger school of literature' on the ground that he was 'hot, soft and woolly'. We had most of us never seen her before but were much impressed with her appearance and the vigour of her repartees to those who were brave enough to cross swords with her. Whether she was a great poetess or merely an original, few of us were competent to say. We admired her vigour but thought a little ridiculous the manner in which the family always insisted on speaking together and rebutting as a family the attacks that were made on any of them. Were they three persons or only one?

Shortly afterwards Harold went with some friends to Edith's recitation of *Façade* at the Aeolian Hall. There were two masks—one black and one white. Osbert Sitwell announced the titles of the poems through the black mask and Edith recited them through the white. William Walton accompanied. It was a strange performance. Some of the audience tittered, but Harold was moved as the performance finished with his favourite 'Beelzebub'.

The two undergraduate poets of these years were Harold Acton who had, as I have said, his book *Aquarium* in actual publication, and Peter Quennell who had come up from Berkhamsted along with the Headmaster's son Graham Greene, to Balliol and who also had published his volume, which had won for him high praise and comparison with Swinburne and Shelley. Louis Golding was, as far as I recollect, the only other undergraduate with a published book to his credit—a novel—and he, older than Harold or Peter Quennell, was a *revenant* from before the war and was in no way in their sets. Peter Quennell was a devotee of Rupert Brooke and, though they were good enough friends he and Harold, Georgian and anti-Georgian, were not really of the same temperament. Quennell had his friends and those who spoke highly of him, but his interests were never really in Oxford and he neither played nor had any desire to play any part in the formation of the Oxford of the 1920's at all comparable to that of Harold Acton. Balliol was to him but a stepping-stone to London and the Café Royal and he had, I fancy, already come to despise his own poetic talents.

The undergraduate verse of the day was collected in yearly volumes known as *Oxford Poetry*. F. W. Bateson, their editor, attempted to con-scribe both Harold and Peter to help him in their production, but their tastes were too antipathetic to one another and the collaboration was not happy. Harold was *par excellence* a social figure, his time mainly spent at parties or societies, at all times ready to read through his megaphone his own poems or those of T. S. Eliot to any passer-by. His official work he did not take at all seriously. Roy Harrod was his tutor and his nominal study was economics. He went to him from time to time to read high-flown essays, but Roy Harrod decided—and Harold did not dissent—that he had little capacity for economics since he was unable to under-stand why it should be an objection to a proposition that he had a few sentences before asserted the exact contrary.

Such times as he did not devote to social activities he spent largely at the theatre. He did not belong to the University Dramatic Society—the OUDS—and was not himself an actor, but J. B. Fagan had just estab-lished the Oxford Repertory Company where Elissa Landi was making her name as an actress and Harold was a frequenter of its plays. His chief friendship among the Dons was with Jacky Beazley, the supreme authority on Greek vases. With him and with Mrs Beazley, with whom he had made friendship when he took off his hat to her goose he was a frequent visitor at the Judge's lodgings just outside the House, where they lived, and he later went with them to Spain.

The closest of his companions at Eton had been Brian Howard but at Oxford they drifted apart. Howard in his passion for the aristocracy, which he combined with a profession of Communist opinions, came to transfer his interests from poetry to horses. At Oxford the closest of Harold's companions was Evelyn Waugh. They went about constantly together. Afterwards their relations had to some extent their ups and downs but appreciation and mutual regard were in general maintained.

They were the two dominating figures at Oxford—Harold, though in years the younger, the more dominating Evelyn did not dispute his predominance. Harold only regretted in Evelyn his lack of musical appreciation and was unable to share his taste for beer. We all used to meet together, as has been said, in Evelyn's rooms in Hertford for a luncheon of cheese and beer. I remember Harold sitting there in the midst of the beer-bibbers, incongruously drinking water. Though by no means a teetotaller he never drank as Evelyn drank and when he drank, like an Italian he drank wine. His habits of careful dress were always a little bewildered by the extravagant untidiness and eccentricity—not to say, dirt—of Evelyn's friend, Terence Greenidge.

Immediately after they went down from Oxford both Evelyn and Harold went through periods of apparent lack of success and found themselves not quite the dominating figures that they had been in their undergraduate days. For Evelyn, as has already been recorded, it was the period of his undistinguished schoolmastering activities, culminating in the attempt to drown himself off the Welsh coast. For Harold it was the period of discovery that there was no possibility of living entirely as a poet, as had till then been his ambition. His new volume of poems, *An Indian Ass*, was not a great success. His father, though a great lover and collector of objects of art, had no great interest in writing and thought it a waste of time. Somerset Maugham had not much greater opinion of the importance of other than his own writing and a little callously advised Harold's father that if his son insisted on being a poet, the best plan was to 'give him a hundred and fifty pounds and tell him to go to hell'. Harold decided that the only way to make a literary career was to write a novel. It was not a form of art for which he had any natural predisposition. He settled down to write his novel *Humdrum* but to do so was against the grain and the novel had no great success.

Evelyn Waugh's *Decline and Fall* came out at the same time as Harold's *Humdrum* and was received with immensely greater approval. At Evelyn's first marriage, which was in an Anglican Church, Harold was his best man. 'A Roman Catholic, are you? I'm afraid that you'll find this all a little stark,' said the vicar to him of the ceremony. Evelyn dedicated *Decline and Fall* to Harold. Evelyn's fame then grew and according to his report Harold was at the time a great victim of jealousy. Evelyn found it difficult to know how to approach him. 'I don't know what to say,' he complained to me one day. 'If I tell him that I am going to lunch at the Ritz, he says "Of course you're a famous author but you can't expect a nonentity like me to join you there." If I suggest that we should go to a pub, he says, "My dear, what affectation—a popular novelist going to a pub." What can I propose?'

Of course as success followed success with Evelyn's early novels his fame in the public eye soon came very greatly to outrun that of Harold. Yet, whatever his passing jealousy, Harold's abundant good humour soon reasserted itself. He abandoned his ambition to be a poet and was content enough to live mainly abroad—to cultivate such friends as Norman Douglas which Florentine life brought to him—and no longer greatly cared whether his name was frequent in the English papers. With the 1930's he went out to China and found great happiness in the life there, lecturing to his beloved students at the University. But the life there meant of course that he for the time passed completely out of the life of Evelyn and of Oxford and he abdicated from what the gossip columns would recognise as achievement.

Neither of the two had, as I have said, any natural liking for politicians whom they considered as an almost inevitably uncultured crew. We have already seen Harold Acton's low opinion of Brendan Bracken whom he considered—not altogether justly—as an archetype of the unpleasant fixer. It is generally considered that the Canadian Rex Mottram in Evelyn's *Brideshead Revisited* was also based on Bracken. He is an uncouth adventurer of a similar type—a Canadian where Bracken had been, as we thought, an Australian by origin. If Mottram was intended to be a portrait of Bracken it is not in fact entirely a just portrait. Bracken may have been at bottom a vulgarian and an adventurer but he cannot be accused of being an appeaser in British pre-war politics. Nor is it unthinkable that he might have wished to be reconciled to the Catholic Church—as in his case the process would have been—in order to facilitate some desirable marriage or for some worldly reason. Such a thing never happened, but, had it happened, he certainly would not have been found guilty of the absurdly naïve beliefs about Catholic teaching which Evelyn ascribes to Mottram. Whatever his faults Bracken was far from ignorant and unread. Yet however much the two of them may have disliked politicians and however much they may have preferred that political conflict should not invade their aesthetic life, the interwar years rapidly took on themselves a shape in which it was no longer possible for any sane man to escape from political attitudes. Evelyn did so as long as he could. To begin with he had no hostile reaction towards Mussolini and on the whole supported him in his war against Abyssinia. He supported Franco in Spain and was only, among totalitarian regimes, irretrievably hostile to Hitler's Nazis. Harold's record was on the whole more easily coherent. With no natural interest in politics or liking for politicians he had no sympathy with the fashion of the day among intellectuals to give support to the Left. 'I don't know much about politics,' he said at the time of the General Strike on seeing some dockers down in Rotherhithe, 'but I can't help feeling that if these people should get into power it would not be a very good thing for art.'

'Undergraduates recur,' as we have already quoted from Warden Spooner. The laureates go down. Acton and Quennell departed from Oxford and their places were taken by such as Auden, Spender, Day-Lewis and MacNeice, who were all dedicated to political commitment. Auden who at that date was the best known among the younger generation was especially politically inclined. Betjeman alone among the younger Oxford poets was immune to this temptation. I first met Auden at dinner with Roy Harrod when he had just gone down and was for the time earning his living as a private schoolmaster. I was told then that the scholarship papers of aspiring young candidates were filled with quotations from his works. I found him, as indeed I always found him, a very agreeable young man, though inclined to smoke too much. In later years when we had both come to other interests we shared together a great admiration for G. K. Chesterton about whom we both had written.

Harold had the advantage over other young writers of the day, whether of the Right or of the Left, that he took political sides not through any political ambitions or theoretical desire for political commitment but because he came to dislike totalitarianism through personal experience, like the negro in Alabama who, when asked by a too enthusiastic evangelist whether he believed in baptism replied, 'Why, sure, boss, I seen it done.' Before the Fascist seizure of power he had proclaimed himself a supporter of Dom Sturzo's *Partito Popolare* but he had never had any especial admiration for or interest in the old Italian Parliamentary politicians nor did Mussolini and the Fascists in their early days especially interfere with the rhythm of the life of his cultured family circle. He was no expert on social problems nor greatly interested in them, but he felt from the first that a totalitarian regime was a threat to that free cultural interchange which was so essential to decent living. The absurd game of refusing to refer to Mussolini by his name at table and calling him instead Mr Smith for fear that spying servants might overhear and delate their masters was to his mind degrading and disgusting. Had he lived in Germany he would doubtless have found the Nazi regime even worse than the Fascist, but he was content with what he knew from personal experience and was under no temptation, like Evelyn and some of the rest of us, to express any approval of the Abyssinian invasion.

Increasingly disillusioned with inter-war Europe he thought to find a spiritual home in China where he lived during the 1930's. He learnt from that experience a deep and abiding hatred of the Japanese who were at that time invading China. With the European war he discovered that, in spite of his Italian and American connections his primary loyalty was to England and after some difficulty he obtained a commission in the RAF. It was his ambition to be posted to China but, owing to some unsavoury and libellous private reports on his conduct, he was never allowed to reach that country, getting only as far as India. On his way to the East he was torpedoed near the Azores on the *Llangibby Castle* and thought for a time that he would drown. The survivors were huddled together on a wet, sloping deck, where Harold found himself 'next, my dear, to a very pretty little Squadron Leader' and they were eventually rescued by a Dutch tug and towed into Horta-Faial.

It was after the war that he and Evelyn found themselves once more in one another's frequent company. They found themselves together in Los Angeles whither Evelyn had gone with the hope that *Brideshead Revisited* might be made into a film. The film was never made but the journey produced *The Loved One*, Evelyn's highly satirical account of the funeral homes of Forest Lawns. What seemed to him the barbarities of American life that was based on no tradition of culture, utterly disgusted Evelyn. Harold was not insensitive to the degree of justice in Evelyn's strictures. He was as conscious as Evelyn of the absurdity of the worship of mechanical devices, most of which in no sort of way ministered to the convenience of life. He sympathised with Evelyn when at New Orleans, being told by the manager of his hotel that 'owing to the air-conditioning system there was no way of opening the window of his bedroom', Evelyn took up his stick and broke the window. On the other hand Harold had many American relatives to whom he was devoted. He had after the war paid serious attention to the plea of a favourite uncle that he should become an American citizen and he knew of both his relatives and other Americans of whom a charge of total lack of culture could not by any stretch of language be justified. He therefore was not ready wholly to accept Evelyn's unbridled strictures and for his failure received from him much abuse. 'The trouble with you,' said Evelyn to him 'is that you're really a Yank' and, hearing that Harold was writing his *Memoirs*, said as they parted, 'This is probably the last time that I shall speak to you.'

Happily it by no means proved to be so. A few years later in 1952 when Evelyn was to visit Italy he wrote to suggest that Harold should accompany him on a trip round the country. Harold agreed, but was somewhat perturbed by Evelyn's growing eccentricities. Thus they visited the Capuchin catacomb near Palermo where the mummies of the dead friars are permanently preserved. Evelyn remained in contemplation of the mummies an inordinately long time and at last emerged, pronouncing on them the verdict that their smell was 'delicious'. It had, he claimed, completely cured the lameness from which he had been suffering and he at once threw away the stick with whose aid he had up till then been walking. Their trip was on the whole a success but was marred by a *contretemps* in a restaurant in Verona when Evelyn with excessive rudeness attacked a young Californian whom he did not at all know but who had entered the restaurant in a dirty chintz-like shirt open at the neck and without a collar or tie. 'Madam,' he said to the boy's mother, 'we haven't been introduced and I don't care where you come from. When he enters a decent restaurant your son should be properly dressed.' Harold was always careful to be polite to waiters and to keep on good terms with them. For this Evelyn rebuked him, arguing that such familiarity was degrading. He was by then fairly clearly developing all those eccentricities which in a few years were to be recorded in *The Ordeal of Gilbert Pinfold*.

In his late years Harold had withdrawn his interest more or less from any concern with the active politics of the day and given himself to the study and on the whole rehabilitation of the much-abused Neapolitan Bourbons. He quotes from Blake, 'He who would do good must do it in minute particulars. General good is the plea of the scoundrel, hypocrite and flatterer.' Whether his attempts to rehabilitate these monarchs have been successful or whether in his ambition for a colourful story he has too much overlooked the miseries of their subjects it is no business of this book to inquire. Realistic in his judgments on the politics of his own day and his own experience, he did not so fully attempt to control his imagination when it played upon the events of the past, sometimes perhaps preferring the plumage to the dying bird. I remember giving dinner shortly after his Oxford days to him and Lord Devlin. Lord Devlin ventured to express his pleasure in Lytton Strachey's *Elizabeth and Essex* which had recently appeared. 'Oh, how can you say that?' exclaimed Harold—'that wicked book which said such fearful things about the Spanish Inquisition which was *so* kind?' Exaggerated or not, at least his work has been most properly rewarded by her Majesty by a well-deserved knighthood.

Harold's father had been brought up as a Catholic but had early lost his faith and never practised his religion, though he had no particular hostility to it. The result was that, when Harold went to Eton, his father was content enough that he should follow the official and nominally Anglican regimen and attend the College Chapel, though he showed no especial interest whether or not he believed in the doctrines that he was taught. To Harold with his Italian background Protestantism always seemed impossibly dreary and opposed to reason and he soon demanded that he be allowed to become a Catholic. His father was indifferent but agreeable. His tutor was a stout and not very intelligent Anglican clergyman, C. O. Bevan, who had previously been a master at Sherborne where he had been a great friend of the football fanatic, the Bull, the master so vividly depicted by Alec Waugh in *The Loom of Youth*. By an odd quirk C. O. Bevan shared digs with Aldous Huxley who was also a master at Eton at that day, even though Harold does not seem ever to have discovered that Aldous was lodging in the House that he had to visit. Bevan intensely resented Harold's requests that he should go up to Windsor to receive Catholic instruction from the priest there, Canon Longinotto. But he could not well forbid it. Harold's first published poem appeared in Chesterton's *New Witness*. Lines in it were:

> Oh, what have I to do with thee,
>     Thou pallid, pallid crucifix
> For I am weak and thou art strong.

It would be impertinent to attempt an estimate of the exact nature and depth of his faith whether in Oxford days or later. It is only in a peculiar atmosphere that risqué jokes, whether of smut or blasphemy, seem funny. To a generation which has wholly rejected all traditional inhibitions such protests are merely tedious and, if much repeated, unendurable. But the 1920's was a generation when boys had generally come from schools where they had been given nominally Christian instruction and where they had been marched regularly to the school chapel. On the other hand they had generally ceased to believe what they had been taught. They had sufficient substratum of faith, for mild blasphemy against it to seem daring and therefore amusing.

In a society in which matrimonial fidelity was generally accepted as the norm, adulterous violations of it were exciting. To a totally permissive society which takes fornication for granted as the inevitable satisfaction of animal desires without any question of affection playing any part in the operation, it is crude, and unexciting.

To Harold deep, real blasphemy had no attractions. On the other hand he had been brought up in the company of an Italian hagiography where the pious told one another far-fetched tales about little-known saints, neither much knowing nor much caring whether what they told had any historical basis. Shortly after going down Harold had the plan to write a book of *Lives of the Saints,* and did it in satirical form and after the mocking manner of Norman Douglas. Thus he wrote of St Nicholas of Lyra:

> This babe of senile parents proved his worth
> Before his weaning on his day of birth.
> Lo, in his bath he rises and he stands
> And thanks Almighty God with upraised hands,
> For granting Mother such delivery.
> With self-denial grave in infancy
> He fasted, took the breast but twice a week.
> Through psalms and orisons he learnt to speak.
> Sifting through spiritual to earthly things
> His brain's rich hive replenished from the springs
> Of Scripture's honey; the Apocalypse
> Was myrrh to smell and nectar to his lips
> His parents, when such bliss succeeds their pain,
> Henceforth from carnal intercourse abstain.

To Harold the world was a god-inhabited place and he had nothing but contempt for the insufficient explanations of the universe which were offered by the sheer materialists. On the other hand he was very indifferent to the petty rulings of theologians and did not care much whether what they said in detail was true or not. 'Oh, my dear,' he once said, 'I have to do things which I cannot confess,' and in another mood he commented on the delicious frisson of exaltation which he experienced on coming out of the confessional. 'It's worth it,' he said. 'It's worth everything,' and, in pity to a Protestant friend, 'My dear, what you miss.' He greatly horrified the very rigid Mrs Woodruff, mother of Douglas Woodruff, by saying to her one day, 'Oh, but, you know, the Church is coming round to Marie Stopes'—a judgment that would not today be held so bizarre as it was fifty years ago.

Yet any conclusions of his insincerity would certainly be false. I remember one day—as it happened, in Peter Quennell's rooms in Balliol—when, having heard some gossip of my intention to join the Catholic Church he spoke to me in most moving and sincere congratulations, 'It is the only thing in the world,' he said, 'that has a message for everybody from the humblest skivvy to the greatest poet.' His later experience of the brutality of totalitarian regimes certainly increased his conviction of the emptiness of a life that has no place for religion and of the difficulty of believing that Man has an all-important part in the creation unless one can also believe that God became Man.

He had, as I say, no curiosity for the metaphysics of exact definitions. Pasteur's simple faith of the Breton peasant woman attracted him more. He once said that he never had any difficulty in believing in miracles. He doubtless did not know very much about Protestant beliefs, but they had little attraction for him. Puritan habits he abhorred and the claim of any body other than the Catholic Church to represent Christianity seemed to him with his Italian culture self-evidently ridiculous. He found much to admire, during his time in China, in Buddhist teachings about resignation and the conquest of insane desire and ambition, and the closing words of his *Memoirs* gave expression of his belief that Buddhism and Christianity had much to teach each other. He quotes from Madame Lo Chiang, 'A believer both in Christ and in Buddha, you harmonise in yourself their various teachings'. And in this he wrote, 'Her intuition has penetrated one of my cherished ideals. Towards this harmony I still continue to strive,' but where the choice has to be made it must unhesitatingly be made for Christ. He quotes from Valéry's *Le Cimetière Marin* and emphasises Valéry's almost Buddhist insistence on resignation and the vanity of desire, the impermanence of all created things. But his final demand was that in spite of all, '*Le vent se lève. Il faut tenter de vivre*', and Harold notes this as the distinction between Christian and Buddhist teaching.

On the other hand he did not much mix with his fellow undergraduate Catholics at Oxford. They for the most part—incidentally then very many fewer in number than they are today—were well-to-do young men from the Catholic public schools. They had been well drilled by the Jesuits and monks in what was considered the practice of their religion. That is to say, they knew that they had to abstain from sexual adventure before marriage and marriage was to them so far distant that this seemed virtually a total prohibition. They had to abstain from eating meat on a Friday and to attend Mass on a Sunday. These obligations were for the most part punctiliously fulfilled. On the other hand Christ permitted them to drink and to bet. To abstain from such activities was the mark of the Puritan on their superiority to whom they greatly prided themselves, and most of them in the days of Belloc and Chesterton thought it a high point of honour to get drunk from time to time in order to prove the reality of their Catholic faith. They had been brought up exclusively in the company of their co-religionists and many of them had hardly met a Protestant or a non-believer before they came up to Oxford. Of the solid difficulties of the faith they knew nothing and their preceptors at school had done little to encourage them to think out the answers to such difficulties, fearing that in any challenge with the unbelievers they were likely to be worsened and all too probably to lose their faith. It was best to let simple faith alone. It was not thought particularly desirable to introduce them too closely to Catholic thinking or Catholic art. It was safer to stick to rugby football and to talk about who won last Saturday's match. The Continent was to them merely a place for summer holidays. It never occurred to them that real people lived there or live men who wrote books.

Now obviously Harold, brought up in his Italian and artistic circles, accustomed from earliest boyhood to mix impartially with Christians and unbelievers, familiar with the names of all great Continental artists and architects, had very little in common with those young English lay Catholics. Catholic as he was himself, none of his Oxford companions were of the faith. Of the undergraduates of the day the one who most closely rivalled his interests was Jean de Menasce, a very able Levantine who had written a monograph called *Since Cézanne*. Though Menasce afterwards became a Catholic and indeed died as a most edifying Dominican, he was by no means at that time religious, being rather as he once wrote to me, fairly or unfairly, a disciple of 'aestheticism of the worst sort'. The Catholic society was the Newman Society which met on Sunday evenings under the auspices of Monsignor Barnes, its chaplain. Harold did not frequent its meetings. He did indeed read one paper to that society—about British genre painters, such as Wilkie, Frith, Augustus Egg and Martineau. I did not happen to hear it, and what the company made of it in Harold's treatment I cannot guess. I think few of them knew very much of the painters discussed before the paper and doubt if they knew very much more after.

# Oxford since the Twenties

'Can this be Oxford? This the place?'
(He cries) of which my father said
'The tutoring was a damned disgrace,
The creed a mummery, stuffed and dead?'
*Dedicatory Ode*—Hilaire Belloc

The total interruption of the war would have made it inevitable in any event that after the war there should be revision and reconsideration of what modifications were required in the Oxford system to meet the new conditions. Oxford immediately after the war was overcrowded as the troops returned from the trenches to jostle for rooms with the boys straight from school. Yet the returning soldiers would soon be gone. Was this overcrowding then but a temporary problem? Or would a larger number demand a University education than before the war? Many of the Dons had hoped for a return to pre-war numbers and pre-war conditions. Were there not the new Redbrick Universities to which the new generation who aspired to education could conveniently go? Why could not Oxford become again the Oxford which it had been in the happy days before 1914? Yet, however much the Dons might wish it, the new post-war England was not content that things should go on exactly as they had been before. Women had been at Oxford for some time before the war but had not as yet been allowed to receive degrees. With some reason that compromise was by the post-war world voted absurd, at a time when women—at least those above 30—were given their parliamentary vote. There might be something to be said for a single-sex Oxford of tradition—for excluding women altogether from the place and either denying them University education or giving them their own University at some other place—as some said, at Bletchley, half-way between Oxford and Cambridge. It was hard to think of any sane argument for admitting their physical presence, allowing them to sit and pass the examinations but denying them degrees. The post-war world with comparatively little opposition removed this anomaly and gave them degrees. Yet it still imposed irritating restrictions on them, under the excuse that every precaution must be taken that the city should not be littered with illegitimate babies. The excuse was made both by Dons and by undergraduates to excuse their own prejudices. Absurder Dons, like Landon at Trinity and Cruttwell at Hertford, attempted to keep the atmosphere of their lectures pure by peppering the women with obscenities so long as they continued to attend. The undergraduates, no more generous, refused to admit them to the Union and their other societies.

The total monopoly of all English education by Latin and Greek no longer survived. At schools other subjects—History, Science, Modern Languages and the like—were now admitted, though only admitted as inferiors and of far lesser esteem than the full Classical curriculum. Still a proportion of schoolboys now left school, having learnt no Greek. Was it sensible to exclude them from Oxford by making Greek a compulsory subject for matriculation? The battle was fought out with some bitterness in Congregation. The advocates of the old ways argued that the decline of Greek in the schools was a great tragedy and that it would decline still further if Oxford no longer insisted on it as a compulsory subject. More enlightened classicists like Maurice Bowra joined with the moderns and argued that on the contrary no sensible purpose was served by compelling unwilling boys to mug up just enough Greek to pass an entrance examination and that Greek learning would be the gainer if Greek was only demanded of those who really wanted to learn the language fully.

The abolitionists eventually won. So the end of the war compelled Oxford to meet a number of questions. Many of those questions had existed for years in any event, but Dons are adepts at evading the answers to inconvenient questions. It might well have been that even now they would have avoided the questions. The crisis that compelled them to meet them was financial. Up till now the University, or rather the Colleges, had managed their own financial business. The Colleges had their landed possessions. They differed greatly from one another in endowed incomes, from Christ Church and Magdalen with, according to Rose and Ziman's *Camford Observed* £133,732 and £105,442 down to Exeter with a mere £21,759. Some of the most important of them such as Balliol had only very moderate incomes. Yet with their

incomes they were able to live on their own. They charged their undergraduates. They subsidised those fees out of their own incomes. They
offered financial scholarships to those who could earn them by examination. They made small contributions to finance the central funds of the
University which had the duty of awarding degrees, examining for the
public examinations and keeping such order as might be necessary in
the streets by the agency of the Proctors.

After the war the Colleges' incomes were wholly insufficient to maintain themselves and the University. There were only two possibilities.
Either Oxford must cease to perform the functions which it had been
performing or else more money must be found. The first possibility was
by general agreement wholly unacceptable. So there was nothing for it
but to get more money. Appeals for charitable support would clearly be
quite insufficient, and even if sufficient could have been obtained, would
have left the University the property of rich benefactors—of the hard-
faced men who had done so well out of the war—to a degree that would
have been wholly undesirable. It could only be obtained from the State.
Therefore a commission was set up under Mr Asquith to settle the terms
of the State's assistance. Now Asquith had been the most brilliant and
successful of the University's undergraduates in the late years of the
previous century. He had won every prize and honour which the University had to offer. He loved and revered the place and for all his liberalism
was as unwilling as Mr Gladstone had been to see any of its ancient
customs changed. Laughing critics in the House of Commons used to
say that, when as Prime Minister, he had a post to offer, the only question
in which he took any interest was what class the applicant took in his
final schools at the University. The whole system was to him perfect. If
Oxford (and of course Cambridge) needed money the State should give
them money but should exact no price for their subvention. It should be
as far as possible a free gift. The most distinguished Oxford man among
his political supporters was Sir John Simon who was mainly interested
that there should be no abridgement from the peculiar privileges of All
Souls of which he was a Fellow. Therefore the Asquith commission
made a recommendation of a financial grant to the Universities but made
few other recommendations for change or reform. The Dons were for
the most part delighted.

Yet the matter could not be so easily settled and once the University
had become financially dependent on the State it was inevitable, whether
Asquith and the Dons wished it or not, that before long certain other
questions about how that money was to be spent should be asked. If we

were writing a history of Oxford University since the First World War obviously we would have to spend a considerable space in describing what changes were introduced or advocated. With the complications of College finance and University finance it is not easy to give a crude figure of the public contribution to the Universities' finance and Oxford's figures are a great deal harder to disentangle than those of Cambridge, but in 1960–61 out of a total income of £4,960,000 the Government grant to Cambridge was £3,970,000 and undergraduates' fees, of which the greater part came from public funds through Local Education Authorities, were a further £450,000. The contribution has, like every-thing else, risen over the years. In the year 1974–5 the grant to Oxford was £15,000,000. In the financial year ending July 31, 1976, the University's income was £18,000,000 and the Government Grant £17,264,000.

For the moment our concern is with the Oxford undergraduates of the 1920's and with what they talked about, and, as I look back, I can only record that it is truly extraordinary how little they talked about such subjects. As I have said, all the undergraduates with whom I associated had been at one or other of the public schools. They did not particularly support the public school system. They were quite willing to make jokes about it and to agree in theory that it would be only fair that Oxford's doors should be thrown open to boys from less distinguished schools. But by what means this career should be thrown open to 'Birmingham, etc.' we never seriously considered and I hardly ever remember hearing it seriously discussed. I think that we would vaguely have thought that all places should be thrown open to free examination—in other words that the Colleges should consist solely of scholars. But when in the nine-teenth century examination tests were more freely introduced both at the Universities and in the Civil Service there were those, like Anthony Trollope, who argued that under the old system of nomination a poor boy could sometimes be preferred to a rich boy but that under a system of universal examination the boys from certain favoured schools would undoubtedly be much better prepared than the boys from the schools that were less favoured and as a result would win more places. Thus equality of opportunity would by no means be obtained. This is to a large extent what has happened, until today some Colleges frankly confess that they mark the papers of candidates from comprehensive schools more generously than those of boys from independent schools, finding that the only way in which they can get a reasonable proportion of them in.

Still, by whatever roads, the composition of the undergraduate population and indeed of the Dons has changed over the years—perhaps not as greatly as some would have thought desirable—but it has certainly changed. Have those changes been for good or for bad? Is it the merely nostalgic sentimentality of an old man which imagines that some of the magic of Oxford, which Matthew Arnold so lovingly praised has gone with the demands of modern necessity and with the decline of the sense of the past and of tradition? It was in the halcyon years before 1914 that that magic was most strongly felt. It was well before then that Quiller Couch wrote:

> Know you her secret none can utter,
>   Hers of the Book, the triple Crown
> Know you the secret none discover?
>   Tell it—when *you* go down.

or Belloc:

> The Freshman ambles down the High,
>   In love with everything he sees.
> He notes the racing autumn sky,
>   He sniffs a lively autumn breeze.

Does the sense of magic still survive as strongly in the modern world of demos, schools-cramming and undergraduate self-government in the Oxford where the approaching motorist, looking for the 'dreaming spires', is instead confronted with a hoarding which tells him, 'Oxford, Home of Pressed Steel?'

As for Dons, they drink less, probably work more, certainly are more frequently divorced. They speak on television whenever they can. Otherwise I do not know that their habits have changed so much over the last fifty years. The intrigues of academic politics, more bitter than any other politics, are much what they have always been. Students of Lord Snow have recently been given a vivid picture of the strange in-fighting of academic life in his account of the battles for the election of the Head of a College (at Cambridge, it is true, but it might just as well have been at Oxford). I do not know that the spirit in which the battle was fought differs very much from that in which the Fellows of Lincoln banded together to keep Mark Pattison out of the Rectorship of that College or in which the Fellows of Balliol attempted to keep out Jowett, or the Z's and the Puseyites combined to conspire against Hampden being elected a Regius Professor. The Dons are no longer, it is true, in Holy Orders, but they have not changed very much by losing their faith.

Of course there have over the years been certain modifications in the curricula of various schools. Such changes were by no means envisaged or advocated by Asquith. What is more to our point is that they were by no means envisaged or advocated by the undergraduates of the 1920's. As I look back on our conversations, we were quite extraordinarily uncritical and incurious about the courses that we were offered. Almost all of us read either Greats or History. We hardly knew that there were such beings as scientists and most of us had no notion where the scientific laboratories might be. We had not the foggiest notion who had settled our curricula or how decisions about it had been arrived at. The constitution of the faculties was unknown to us. Criticism was already beginning to concern itself about the excessive specialisation of English education—the excessive specialisation of the Universities which imposed an excessive and too early specialisation on the schools. The stricter entrance qualification and courses were made at the University in conformity with the demand that Oxford should no longer be a mere playing-field for the idle rich, the greater the pressure on schools to make their pupils specialists in order to get them into and to do well at the University. We poked fun at the curricula of the schools but we had little notion how even those curricula were decided. Maurice Bowra came to know most intimately the workings of the University machine but I doubt if even he knew much about them in his undergraduate days. I do not suppose that any of the rest of us had the faintest idea what a faculty was. When shortly after the war the greekless Greats of PPE were established we knew little about it, had little idea whether it was a good thing or bad, but would in general have been inclined to agree with many of the more old-fashioned Dons that it was a school which no gentleman should read.

In the same way we accepted as a virtue which distinguished Oxford and Cambridge from other Universities in England and elsewhere the College system. One belonged to one's College. It was the College which was responsible for one's work—such as it was. We did not ask ourselves how far the College system was in fact being eroded by the creation of new faculties in strange subjects, whose students had to go outside College for their tutorials, or by the establishment of new chairs, the holders of which were attached to various Colleges without any selection by its reigning Fellows. The University grants when they came to be given were given to the University, not to the individual Colleges.

The importance was by no means generally recognised. Undergraduates still thought of themselves as primarily members of their College. Yet the College, strangely enough, is hardly mentioned in the official record of rules, the Excerpta e Statutis, which is presented to every undergraduate on his matriculation. As a current piece of light verse has it:

> All undergraduates may do
> Their main official duties
> With but a passing reference to
> Excerpta e Statutis

Dons were equally College-bound in their minds. Bursars clamoured for larger numbers in order that they might get more income, the tutors for restricted numbers in order that they might maintain their hold over their pupils. The undergraduates themselves hardly noticed the decline in amenities. Though the pressure of numbers meant that they had to share sitting-rooms on a scale that would have been undreamed of before the war and that guest rooms were markedly less commodious than those at Redbrick Universities, I doubt if anyone at Oxford knew this. Nowhere is one likely to have to walk further to reach a urinal than at an ancient University, not even in the United States. We took these things for granted. We did not discuss them in our conversations.

There was at that time an examination called Divers, by which every undergraduate soon after he came up was compelled to pass an examination on the Acts of the Apostles and one or other of the Gospels. John Betjeman had to take that examination, failed in it and was sent down. Betjeman was enormously popular with us all since we found him the pleasantest and most amusing of men, and we agreed that it was the greatest shame that he should be sent down—the more so that he was a religious fanatic and there was therefore a certain irony in his being failed in a religious examination. But in all our complaints it never occurred, as far as I remember, to anyone to ask who it was that ordained that Divers should be a compulsory examination, nor, when soon after it was abolished, did we ask by whom such abolition was decreed or by what machinery.

The changes that have taken place in Oxford between the 1920's and today, whether they have been for good or bad, have for the most part taken place not through any conscious planning nor through conscious desire but as the inevitable consequence of events. Up till 1914 Oxford and the Colleges were, as we have seen, financially self-supporting. What they did they did out of their own independence. It was not for the State or anybody else to dictate to them. Once they asked for and received Government support it was inevitable that the Government should claim some control over the way in which that money was spent. The Dons would have preferred that they should have handed over the money and then left the Colleges to decide for themselves how it should be spent. The Dons thought that they knew best how a University should be run, but the strange truth is that nowhere is education a subject less honoured or studied than in Universities. The Diploma of Education is the least regarded and least honoured of the University's awards.

Perhaps, all things considered, it is remarkable that the Government, while giving the money, has left the University as much independence as it has. Yet some dictation was inevitable. Science, though still in the opinion of scientists most inadequately provided for in contrast with what happened at other Universities, was provided for a little more generously than in former times. This meant that for financial reasons central University laboratories had to be built to replace the very inadequate College laboratories of Victorian times. The development made an increase in the power of the University at the expense of the Colleges.

The Bridges Syndicate has discovered that, what with science and other new faculties less than half of College teaching is now done by teaching members of the undergraduate's own College. Mr Peter Laslett has argued in a startling broadcast talk that Oxford and Cambridge should cease to take undergraduates at all. All undergraduate courses, he says, should be at one or other of the Redbrick Universities and the student should come to his College at Oxford or Cambridge for his postgraduate work. This would be a very grave affront to all traditions of the place and there is little likelihood of it being adopted in any near future. Besides a lot of valuable postgraduate work is now done at Redbrick Universities, which often specialise in particular subjects that Oxford and Cambridge do not touch. It would be a pity that all such should be suppressed.

Up till 1914 the financial benefits of a scholarship had been all-important. The scholarship was the means by which, and by which alone, the son of poor parents was able to win his way to the University. Since the 1920's and the Government grants the scholarship has been financially of no importance. A democratic government has insisted that no boy who is intellectually qualified should be excluded from a University simply because of his parents' poverty. As a result there is an elaborate system

of grants through means tests imposed by the Local Education Authorities to pay the fees of poorer undergraduates. This means test is equally
applied to scholars and, if their parents are wealthy, scholars are docked
of the emoluments which they have earned by their scholarship. Therefore there is no longer any advantage in a scholarship save the advantage
of prestige for the winner. Is there any purpose served by any longer
holding scholarship examinations and with the awarding of scholarships? The disadvantage is obvious. The desire to prepare candidates
for success in scholarship examinations imposes upon schools an exclusively specialist school curriculum. They become Classical, Mathematical,
History or Science specialists at an unhealthily early age and the pattern
of English education is perverted. To whose advantage? The people who
clamour for the preservation of the scholarship system are the Sixth
Form schoolmasters who gain prestige by their victories and preen
themselves if their pupils win more scholarships than those from a rival
school. But is it worth preserving an evil system to pander to this unhealthily competitive pride?

In the years between the 1920's and the outbreak of the Second World
War there were indeed changes and developments at Oxford, but they
were perhaps not much noticed by most undergraduates and it was on
the whole surprising that they were not greater. The numbers, even after
the returning soldiers had departed, still continued to increase. The
young were still under the impression that if they had University degrees
they would get better jobs. The Redbrick Universities grew in importance.
In the 1920's no one from one of the better public schools would have
dreamed of going to such a place. Now, with entrance qualifications to
Oxford (and Cambridge) much stricter, schools of every type were glad
to get their pupils in at any Redbrick. The courses offered there were as
good as those at Oxford or Cambridge, and indeed the only notable
superiority of the older Universities was in the sporting pages of the
daily papers where their contests were still by far the more extensively
reported—it is not very clear why. New faculties offered new courses
on everything, as is now said, from Plato to NATO but their discoveries
were not in general much noticed. The Union, as is its habit, had its ups
and downs—perhaps the downs more generally noticed, rightly or
wrongly. Its high moment, if not of fame, at least of notoriety was with
the passage of the famous King and Country motion, but the excessive
publicity with which that met must be credited rather to the follies of the
London press and Mr Randolph Churchill than to Oxford or the Union
itself.

The Dons had always preserved the liberal tradition which they had inherited from Jowett. The individual Don might have his opinions, political or religious. The Greats Dons made strangely little attempt to consider the metaphysical claims of the Christian religion. They jumped straight from Aristotle to Descartes with no passing mention of Aquinas or any other scholastic in between. Yet this was no deliberate oversight and in general the Don thought it a point of honour not to let his own political opinions appear in his lectures or his tutorials. Though most of the Dons were agnostics they would have thought it a breach of etiquette to attempt directly to pervert the religious opinions of their pupils. It was only shortly before the war that Richard Crossman at New College began to use his official academic lectures on Plato as frankly political platforms in which, without any pretence of impartiality, he preached his socialistic principles. It was a novel tactic and widely disapproved of by other Dons, not themselves by any means all of Conservative political opinions.

The Second World War of course brought another interruption in the life of Oxford, though an interruption a great deal less drastic than that of twenty-five years before. This time the authorities did not call up boys of eighteen straight from school, but allowed them to start their University careers. Oxford's life was therefore truncated but not altogether interrupted. After the war, in contrast to what happened in the 1920's, and rather to everyone's surprise and even to some old people's slight dismay, undergraduates (and schoolboys) by no means indulged in the anarchic protests against authority which had signalised those of earlier years. They were rather surprisingly submissive, obedient to authority and well-behaved. Why this was so no one quite knew. Perhaps the difference between the two eras was that after 1918 there was a hard-faced coalition government in power, after 1945 a Labour Government. It is the natural habit of youth always to protest against the Government. Therefore after 1918 the young were radicals, after 1945 conservatives. However the backlash, if a little delayed, was eventually inevitable. As we have said, the number of undergraduates immediately after the 1914 war was very large, owing to the returning soldiers coming up to complete their careers. No one could then be certain whether when the soldiers went down the numbers would return to pre-war dimensions or would continue to expand. They did of course expand.

The public schoolboy who came up to the University before or immediately after the war took it for granted that a job would be waiting for him when he went down, should he happen to want it.

There was no fear of unemployment in his class. He obtained such a job in fact not because anybody thought that a University graduate was especially more fitted to the job but because the society was an oligarchic society where jobs were easily available for those with social advantages. But it was not perhaps unnatural that the young should draw the wrong conclusion and decide that the young got jobs not because of their social advantages but because they had gone to the University. Therefore those of them with book-ability clamoured that they too should be admitted to a University. A large number went to the Redbrick Universities. Even boys from public schools who in the early 1920's hardly recognised the existence of Redbrick Universities were now quite content to go to them if they could not win admission to Oxbridge but could pass into one of these other academies. Even the number of those who obtained admission to Oxford and Cambridge increased, though not so markedly. The expectation was, of course, to a degree fulfilled. In the years between the wars, while England still remained to a large extent, and probably more than any other country in the world, a class society, while the English alone preserved their strange taste for putting handles of prefix and suffix to their names and of creating hereditary titles, numbers of young men and women were able through University careers to rise from the ranks and to obtain top jobs—more so than in previous generations. Immediately after the war shortages meant that there was no unemployment and jobs were available for all.

When only a small proportion of the population received University educations it might be that those few got the most desirable jobs. But when a very large proportion of the population received such an education, there were no longer sufficient especially desirable jobs to accommodate them all. Indeed a large part of our unemployment problem today arises from the fact that too many want white-collar jobs and too few are willing to work with their hands. The most that the University graduate can now hope for is a very pedestrian job and the University graduate is less willing to accept such jobs than he who has not got a degree. So the result is that we are seeing the beginning of graduate unemployment as in America. The undergraduate no longer sees any advantage in a University degree and the number of applicants for University entrance is on the decline.

The purpose of policy was ever since the war to see to it that every young person of sufficient ability should be offered a University education and none should be denied simply because of parents' poverty. To some extent this has been achieved, though the friends of egalitarianism still complain that an unduly large proportion of undergraduates come from independent schools and too few from state schools. Still the mixture is certainly different from what it has been in past ages.

What has been the consequence? Let us look at the Union. It was always the complaint of critics of the Union that it was the home of ambitious political aspirants. This mark was certainly set upon it after the 1914 war by Hore-Belisha and the criticism could probably have been made with equal justice of the Union before the First War. Yet the rivalries of the Union were always kept within bounds. The Society had a rule that no canvassing was permitted in its elections for office. It was a rule that was not easy to define or to enforce, and it cannot be denied that candidates and their friends sometimes indulged in solicitations that it would not be easy to deny verged upon the nature of canvassing. When Beverley Nichols was the candidate for the Presidency he approached another undergraduate in a dark alley and, taking him by the arm, said, 'You will vote for me tomorrow, won't you, my dear?' His invitation turned out to be somewhat embarrassing when he found that the fellow undergraduate whom he had approached was Dick Routh, the candidate who was standing against him. Indeed I must confess that when I myself stood for the Presidency my great friend, John Sutro, and other well-wishers indulged in activities that it would not have been very easy to defend against a charge of canvassing had such ever been brought against me. Still such irregularities, when they occurred, were not before the war taken too seriously. I do not think that any election was ever officially challenged, and the Union aspirants, even when they were of different political parties, contrived to remain on tolerably amicable speaking relations with one another. In the changed personnel of Oxford and the Union after the war things went on to begin with after very much the same pattern. Under the very able and, as far as I know, wholly acceptable Presidency of Mr Roger Gray the Union flourished and gained in social prestige. Such strange characters as Mr Kenneth Tynan appeared in its debates. It was not until 1957 that troubles came to a head. Mr Brian Walden was then the President and for the first time the two candidates to succeed him were both Asiatic— Mr Athukathhmudalo from Ceylon and Mr D'Mello from Goa. They conducted against one another campaigns of virulence that would have been quite inconceivable to a European. Brian Walden attempted a little to assuage the tempest but, as so often happens, attempting to make things better, only succeeded in making them worse. He made certain remarks about one of the candidates to the editor of the *Isis* in what he imagined to be a private conversation. The editor printed them and Mr D'Mello made public accusations against him of canvassing. The result was the establishment of an unpleasant precedent and since then there have been a number of occasions when Union elections have been called into public dispute. The prestige of the Union has not been the gainer from such battles.

But apart from accidental developments in various institutions, have undergraduates changed so much over the last twenty years? It is not within my province to say. Human nature does not change very rapidly. The changes are rather in institutions and circumstances. Already well before 1920 the old Victorian notion that the Christian religion could be usefully supported by coercion—by test acts and compulsory chapels and by the expulsion of inconvenient atheists like Shelley—had been abandoned. The Colleges still maintained their chapels, their chaplains and their daily services. But they were not much attended nor much regarded. Most of the undergraduates had very frankly abandoned religion and it was generally taken for granted that perhaps Roman Catholics went to church because, as it was put, they had to, but none others. The Catholic Church discovered at the time of Pius X's campaign against modernism at the beginning of the century that attempts to suppress heretical speculation by delation resulted not in the suppression of heresy so much as in the suppression of all speculation. If it was so dangerous to write and to think the best and the safest plan was not to write or to think at all. So in the smaller world of Oxford the consequence of compulsory religion was that undergraduates tended to lose interest in religion altogether, and a consequence of the death of the last elements of compulsion is that, Catholics apart, there is less formal observance than there used to be. The number of undergraduates who go forward to Holy Orders is incomparably less than it was in the nineteenth century and probably even less than it was in the 1920's. On the other hand, while institutional religion may have declined, there is probably more religious speculation, more curiosity about the 'mystery of things' than there used to be. It is rarer to find that banausic indifference to the great ultimate problems.

Similarly with sex. It is inevitable that the difficult time immediately after puberty, when desire is at its strongest and when for financial and social reasons marriage is not yet possible, will be difficult years and there can never have been a time when those years have been traversed without fairly frequent mishaps. Yet it is precisely during those years that the University has the responsibility for its young people. Whether sexual irregularity was more common in the 1920's than in the 1970's who can say? Certainly it was not very uncommon at either time. Probably with the easier and more frequent intermixing of men and women homosexual activities are less common today than they were fifty years ago and, with the greater availability of contraceptive devices, heterosexual activities more frequent. Who can say? The main difference is in the freedom with which such activities are discussed. Abundant evidence shows that habits in Victorian times were a great deal more irregular than was until recently generally understood, but it was, of course, irregular not so much to do such things as publicly to talk about them. Appearance in the divorce courts was ruinous, but incidental fornication, so long as it was not made public, was not thought unforgivable. In the 1920's at Oxford undergraduates and Dons combined to turn blind eyes. The undergraduates were discreet enough not to make public their activities, the Dons made no attempt to discover what was going on, though they must of course have known well enough in a general way. The great difference of modern times is the appearance of a type of undergraduate—not perhaps a very common type but one distinctly recognisable—who thinks it a point of honour and pride to publicise his activities and to challenge the unwilling Dons to interfere with them. He brazenly preaches the doctrine that a man's morals are his private affair and that the University authorities have no business to interfere with them. The University authorities have no wish thus to interfere but sometimes when publicly challenged they have no alternative but to act. The Rabelaisian maxim of '*Fay ce que vouldras*', as all but the immature must know, is hardly a sufficient answer to all problems. Doubtless we do what we want, but what do we want? As Shakespeare more truly and deeply said, what is 'past reason hunted' is also 'past reason hated'.

Yet the most striking difference between the undergraduate of today and that of the 1920's is certainly the growth of the demand among the undergraduates for self-government. In the 1920's the undergraduates occasionally rioted, but it was the essence of their riots that they were always about nothing—mere ebullience of high spirits. Even Hugh Gaitskell, the most high-minded of undergraduates, was caught climbing into New College after midnight and duly fined a pound by the Warden, H. A. L. Fisher. He took it in good part, as did his parents. He was a friend from Dragon Days at Oxford of John Betjeman, but his parents disliked his friendship, thinking that Betjeman was not of sufficiently high social class.

A result of the difficulties of entrance and of the dependence on

Government grants is the formation among undergraduates of a machinery for self-government and for the ventilation of grievances. Undergraduates today fall into two classes. A few are politically minded, organise themselves into Student Unions (to be distinguished from the traditional Union Society), intrigue against one another for the positions of authority in the Union, sit-in, demonstrate, occupy buildings, demand higher grants and more adequate lodgings. Some even stay up long after their undergraduate careers are finished solely to indulge in student politics—an extraordinary activity hitherto unknown and almost inviting the question whether they should any longer be properly called students. The issues upon which they summon the young to agitate are indeed sometimes legitimate undergraduate interests such as the size of grants or the availability of sufficient lodgings. It is reasonable that the undergraduate should demand a say on his conditions of living, less reasonable that he should expect to decide details of his curriculum or methods of instruction which he has come to the University to be taught rather than to decide. At other times they pass resolutions on general topics such as the war in Vietnam, abortion, or the Common Market, on which there is no call for an undergraduate, qua undergraduate, to have a special opinion. The majority find such activities unattractive. Professor Gillies at Hull University has cogently said that those who agitate for student representation on academic bodies should be compelled as a punishment to attend such meetings, and the suggestion is a sensible one, for certainly to any normal young man no activity could be imagined more boring than that of sitting on a committee for the management of academic affairs. One wonders why anyone should have an ambition to be saddled with such penal chores, and that indeed seems to be the very sensible attitude of the great majority of undergraduates. They think the remedy for their grievances a personal remedy. They do not care for organised activity or for those who organise such activities. They absent themselves from such organisations and keep to their books.

They keep to their books a great deal more closely than most of us did in the 1920's since jobs can no longer be taken for granted and may depend they think—probably wrongly—on academic success. On the other hand they are less ready to entertain themselves than we were twenty-five years ago. Television is no doubt partly responsible for that, but apart from the television at every meeting of a society the paper must now be read by some visitor imported from London. The habit is very different from that of, for instance, the New College Essay Society of my days. Now every week the Union debates are supported by imported visitors. In the 1920's when we took it for granted that there was a job waiting for every undergraduate when he went down, those like Maurice Bowra who fancied a job in the academic world took the trouble to excel in their schools. To the rest of us the social advantages of Oxford were far more important than the academic. A considerable number of the brighter of the undergraduates of the 1920's went down without a degree at all and not much regretting the lack of it. The rest of us were not so wholly indifferent. We looked to what we imagined to be the example of F. E. Smith, who, as we thought, had been able to enjoy every pleasure of life and then by a short spurt at the last moment equip himself with a first-class degree. Either we were not as clever as F. E. Smith or his tactics were not as contemptuous as we had imagined. In any case we were not successful and our last-minute bursts only brought in very moderate degrees.

I do not know that we were more sensible than our youngers—I dare say not—but in any event, I fancy, we lived fuller lives and enjoyed them more. Perhaps there was a half-truth in the old saying of Bishop Mandell Creighton, 'The Universities are a sort of lunatic asylum for keeping the young men out of mischief.'

# Index

SOME OPINIONS OF CHRISTOPHER HOLLIS'S
AUTOBIOGRAPHICAL BOOK
*THE SEVEN AGES*

'It is written with such elegance and style, such easy grace and happy wit, as to merit printing on the finest hand-made paper and binding in the most sumptuous Zaehnsdorf leather . . . his character and his book sparkle throughout; I would not care to know a man who met Christopher Hollis and managed to dislike him, or who read *The Seven Ages* and found it anything but a delight . . . I have rarely read a book with so many opinions in it that was so undogmatic . . . He has had many friends, and the sketches of some of them—Belloc, Waugh, Betjeman, Attlee—are shrewd, original and entertaining; vastly entertaining—the book is sprinkled with enchanting anecdotes.'

Bernard Levin *The Observer*

'He certainly earns remission of 10,000 purgatorial years for providing such entertaining, illuminating and often slyly funny memoirs—English-Catholic-squirearchy whimsies and all.'

Laurence Cotterell *The Times*

'What makes it so agreeable, and indeed important, is the spontaneous discussion and illustration with which he enriches his simple account of his life.'

*The Financial Times*

'His own account of his adventures should be read. There are many excellent anecdotes.'

Anthony Powell *The Daily Telegraph*

'By far and away the best and wisest of this year's autobiographies, and probably next; wise, witty, humane, wholly literate.'

*Methodist Recorder*